D1706229

David Price, MS, CAS

Finding a Lover for Life
A Gay Man's Guide to Finding a Lasting Relationship

Pre-publication
REVIEWS,
COMMENTARIES,
EVALUATIONS...

"This book nicely explores and helps the reader reject many of the negative and self-defeating myths that surround gay relationships, and perhaps more important, the myths that get in the way of developing healthy and stable relationships. The broad and overarching perspective takes into account many of the issues, factors, and considerations that go into finding, developing, and maintaining a healthy and permanent relationship, from self-development to the realities and pitfalls of relationships, to finding and keeping a healthy partner. The interjection of writing exercises provides an especially useful supplement to the text itself, and allows readers to explore their own ideas. In addition, the appendix summarizes and provides a set of thoughtful ideas and exercises.

This book focuses on the personal preparation required to find and form a committed relationship, and Price outlines his ideas and thoughts in a practical, sound, and commonsense manner. A glance at the table of contents will show you exactly how useful the book is, and, frankly, many of the ideas are as practical for straight men and women seeking a permanent and intimate relationship as for gay men. The book is about self-development as much as it is dating and finding a relationship, based on the idea that 'you are who you attract.' "

Phil Rich, EdD, MSW, LICSW
Clinical Director,
Stetson School,
Barre, Massachusetts;
Author, *The Healing Journey*
book series

More pre-publication
REVIEWS, COMMENTARIES, EVALUATIONS . . .

"*Finding a Lover for Life: A Gay Man's Guide to Finding a Lasting Relationship* is a highly readable work that covers the important aspects of meeting and finding a lover for a successful relationship. The author discusses antecedent conditions such as fear of intimacy and other emotional baggage that have, in the past, worked against putting all the necessary pieces in place to better assure finding a partner for life.

Beginning with self-assessments, Price leads the reader through identifying values and qualities that would be desirable in a lover, likely places for meeting suitable prospects for dating, and how to proceed with dating in a structured, effective manner. His plan is divided into the preparation stage, the action stage, and the completion stage. Price is an experienced therapist and personal coach who has counseled many clients who have been unsuccessful in finding suitable relationships. The experience and history he shares with his readers is most valuable."

E. Douglas Norton, PhD
Associate Professor,
Department of Counseling,
Development,
and Higher Education,
University of North Texas,
Denton

Harrington Park Press®
An Imprint of The Haworth Press, Inc.
New York • London • Oxford

Finding a Lover for Life
A Gay Man's Guide to Finding a Lasting Relationship

HAWORTH Gay & Lesbian Studies
John P. De Cecco, PhD
Editor in Chief

In Your Face: Stories from the Lives of Queer Youth by Mary L. Gray

Military Trade by Steven Zeeland

Longtime Companions: Autobiographies of Gay Male Fidelity by Alfred Lees and Ronald Nelson

From Toads to Queens: Transvestism in a Latin American Setting by Jacobo Schifter

The Construction of Attitudes Toward Lesbians and Gay Men edited by Lynn Pardie and Tracy Luchetta

Lesbian Epiphanies: Women Coming Out in Later Life by Karol L. Jensen

Smearing the Queer: Medical Bias in the Health Care of Gay Men by Michael Scarce

Macho Love: Sex Behind Bars in Central America by Jacobo Schifter

When It's Time to Leave Your Lover: A Guide for Gay Men by Neil Kaminsky

Strategic Sex: Why They Won't Keep It in the Bedroom edited by D. Travers Scott

One of the Boys: Masculinity, Homophobia, and Modern Manhood by David Plummer

Homosexual Rites of Passage: A Road to Visibility and Validation by Marie Mohler

Male Lust: Pleasure, Power, and Transformation edited by Kerwin Kay, Jill Nagle, and Baruch Gould

Tricks and Treats: Sex Workers Write About Their Clients edited by Matt Bernstein Sycamore

A Sea of Stories: The Shaping Power of Narrative in Gay and Lesbian Cultures—A Festschrift for John P. De Cecco edited by Sonya Jones

Out of the Twilight: Fathers of Gay Men Speak by Andrew R. Gottlieb

The Mentor: A Memoir of Friendship and Gay Identity by Jay Quinn

Male to Male: Sexual Feeling Across the Boundaries of Identity by Edward J. Tejirian

Straight Talk About Gays in the Workplace, Second Edition by Liz Winfeld and Susan Spielman

The Bear Book II: Further Readings in the History and Evolution of a Gay Male Subculture edited by Les Wright

Gay Men at Midlife: Age Before Beauty by Alan L. Ellis

Being Gay and Lesbian in a Catholic High School: Beyond the Uniform by Michael Maher

Finding a Lover for Life: A Gay Man's Guide to Finding a Lasting Relationship by David Price

The Man Who Was a Woman and Other Queer Tales from Hindu Lore by Devdutt Pattanaik

How Homophobia Hurts Children: Nurturing Diversity at Home, at School, and in the Community by Jean M. Baker

The Harvey Milk Institute Guide to Lesbian, Gay, Bisexual, Transgender, and Queer Internet Research edited by Alan Ellis, Liz Highleyman, Kevin Schaub, and Melissa White

Stories of Gay and Lesbian Immigration: Together Forever? by John Hart

Finding a Lover for Life
A Gay Man's Guide to Finding a Lasting Relationship

David Price, MS, CAS

Harrington Park Press®
An Imprint of The Haworth Press, Inc.
New York • London • Oxford

Published by

Harrington Park Press®, an imprint of The Haworth Press, Inc., 10 Alice Street, Binghamton, NY 13904-1580

Cover design by Marylouise E. Doyle.

Library of Congress Cataloging-in-Publication Data

Price, David, 1960-
    Finding a lover for life: a gay man's guide to finding a lasting relationship / David Price.
        p. cm.
    Includes bibliographical references and index.
    ISBN 1-56023-356-7 (hard : alk. paper)—ISBN 1-56023-357-5 (soft : alk. paper)
    1. Gay male couples—United States 2. Dating (Social customs)—United States. 3. Interpersonal relations—United States. 4. Mate selection—United States. I. Title.

HQ76.2.U5 P78 2001
646.7'7'086642—dc21
                                                                                    00-069715

To my spiritual and life partner, Mike,
who offered inspiration

To my friends and mentors,
Doug, Michael, Dennis, and Mark

To my "family of choice,"
those loving gay, bisexual, lesbian,
and straight people who gave
me love and encouragement

ABOUT THE AUTHOR

David Price, MS, CAS, BS, has been a professional counselor since 1983 and a professional coach since 1995. His BS and MS are in counseling psychology. He has worked in outpatient, private practice, and residential settings. He is a member of the National Council on Sexual Addiction and Compulsivity. A nationally certified counselor, he has worked extensively with gay and bisexual men, addressing sexuality, coming out, health, and relationship issues.

He has developed a dating workshop entitled "Finding a Lover for Life" in which he uses a dating coaching approach with single gay and bisexual men. He has published two professional journal articles in *Sexual Addiction & Compulsivity* and has made numerous professional presentations. He has been in a committed relationship for over seven years. He and his partner reside as a couple in Gardner, Massachusetts.

CONTENTS

**PART I: PREPARATION STAGE—PREPARING
    YOURSELF FOR A LASTING RELATIONSHIP**

**PART II: ACTION STAGE—PUTTING ACTION
    WITH YOUR WISHES**

**PART III: COMPLETION STAGE—FINDING
AND KEEPING A LASTING RELATIONSHIP**

Foreword

So many myths abound in the gay community about relationships. In one of the workshops I lead, I ask participants to state all the myths they have heard about gay relationships and write them on the board. One of the first statements from any group is "Gay relationships don't last" or "They don't exist." After listing them on the board we go back through them one by and one and discuss what is true and what is not true about each myth. Objections always come from group members when I state that these myths are not true. "Oh yeah? Where are these relationships? How do you find one?" are the responses I quickly hear.

In my private practice, I have several men who have never had a relationship with a man that has lasted longer than a few dates. They don't have a clue about how to go about dating and finding the right man. Because of all the shame gay men feel from the cultural victimization of heterosexism, families that have not demonstrated intimacy, few positive role models, and myths about gay men, they become discouraged and resigned to a single and lonely life.

This book is a practical guide for those men. I have longed to be able to hand my clients some manual that would help them with their journey. Now I can! If you are one of those men, know that you are not alone, that it is possible to date and find a lasting relationship. Here you will find practical suggestions and exercises. The author even shares personal stories so you know he's talking from experience and just not pontificating.

One of the myths I always hear in my workshops is "Gay men are promiscuous and not monogamous." David busts that myth in this book by explaining that promiscuity and monogamy are choices and may actually be a part of our lives at different times depending upon how serious we are about finding a lasting relationship. It is about setting priorities in our lives and deciding what we truly want for ourselves, not about resigning to a myth that simply is not true for all gay men. It is a choice.

Further, on the promiscuity topic, David explains sexual addiction and the dangers of falling into compulsive acting-out traps. This has been such a taboo subject for many in our community but here it is in black and white and simply stated for those who may either suffer from addiction or need to know that they don't have to follow the compulsive behavior of others.

David addresses all the other stereotypes that gay men fear are true, as well. What about the ads for "straight appearing/acting men"? Is it wrong to be attracted to someone so much younger (or older) than I am? What about S&M? It's all here with simple, easy-to-read, no-nonsense suggestions.

Thank you, David, for writing the book my clients have been anxious to read. May you, the reader, also find this to be a practical guide to your journey for a meaningful relationship. To quote a saying in many Twelve-Step fellowships, "Take what you can use and leave the rest."

Joe Amico, MDiv, CAS, CSAC
Phoenix, Arizona

Introduction

The Process of Preparation
in Finding a Long-Term Partner

If I had eight hours to chop down a tree, I would spend six hours
sharpening the blade and two hours chopping down the tree.

Abraham Lincoln

Your decision to buy this book conveys a powerful statement about
changes in our society and the gay community. You are part of a
growing awareness that a specific process of preparation is required
to enter into a healthy relationship. The view that a person needs to
prepare to find and keep a mate is a relatively new one. Mental health
professionals, lawyers, judges, mediators, ministers, and others who
deal with relationship problems are also realizing the truth of this perspective. Preparation creates an intention that motivates your thinking and behavior concerning your desire to find a lasting relationship.

The view that an individual must prepare for a healthy and lasting
relationship is contrary to most of the common understandings about
relationships. Our culture supports a perspective that relationships
develop through a mysterious process of love and romance. This cultural perspective creates a "fantasy mentality" based on romantic desire. This perspective is supported by the sales of romantic music,
books, and movies. The "romance model of relationships" is the
dominant perspective on relationships in our society. A realistic and
conscious perspective of dating and relationships is often not portrayed in the dominant culture.

You have heard the songs and seen the movies that herald the perspective that "love just happens." A myth exists in our culture that
you just need to find the "right person" and everything will be won-

derful. At any moment fate will bring you together, all of your problems will disappear, and you will instantly be happy. You will know you have found the right person and no other information will be needed. Fireworks will go off, wedding bells will ring, and all will be goodness and light. You and your perfect mate will join together in total and eternal bliss and walk happily into the sunset. This romantic perspective makes great songs and movies, but it is the worst approach to finding a compatible mate and a lasting relationship.

The belief in romantic love is a prevalent belief, but it can also be one of the most damaging. A great deal of pain and disappointment is caused when this belief is found to be untrue. Experience often shows that most relationships based on romance only end. Little evidence exists to prove that the romantic approach works. Many people blame marriage for the failure of the romantic relationship. This failure is not the fault of marriage. The faulty belief that romance is enough to create a lasting relationship is to blame.

The failure of many relationships is the result of a lack of preparation. Many individuals in our society and the gay community are gaining awareness of the faulty learning that has caused this failure. You have the opportunity to be spared the anguish of these mistaken beliefs about romantic relationships. The process of preparing for a lasting relationship involves a period of growth prior to committing to a partner. Abraham Lincoln stated, "If I had eight hours to chop down a tree, I would spend six hours sharpening the blade and two hours chopping down the tree." Preparation is an essential key to a successful relationship.

Let's look for a moment at how the members of the gay community have grown as a culture over the past few decades. The 1960s heralded a time of liberation from established tradition and allowed the free expression of "sexual freedom." In an adolescent fashion, many people in the gay community grabbed onto this concept and interpreted sexual freedom as "I can have any type of sex I want, with whomever I want, any time I want, any way I want, and any place I want. No one can take away that right." This new freedom allowed many to accept their homosexuality, but it also led to sexual promiscuity and a loss of values. Relationships took a backseat to sexual expression and sexual diversity. Sexual freedom was considered the peak of the gay community's "coming of age."

The 1970s saw a great increase in "coming out." Gay men and lesbians announced their homosexuality and took pride in their sexuality. Gay businesses, bars, restaurants, and churches began to emerge. The development of a distinct "gay culture" and "gay identity" emerged. This gay culture allowed many men and women to find a place where they were accepted and belonged. However, many businesses catered to gay and lesbian people simply to obtain their business. Many gay men and lesbians were exploited. Some people joined this visible gay world and thought that being part of it was enough. Others were engaged in relationships, but these individuals were rarely monogamous. Many prominent people in the gay community claimed that homosexual relationships were "different" from heterosexual relationships, and that they did not need to be monogamous or committed to be successful. This was a period of rebellion from the general heterosexual society. The gay community was establishing a separate identity.

In the 1980s, the gay community faced HIV infection and AIDS, and it experienced incredible losses and sadness. As a community, it entered into a long grieving process. Many people reacted negatively to the health crisis and the promiscuous sexuality that had allowed this infection, and there was an increase in sex education and support for "safe sex." Awareness of sexual addiction and compulsivity and the high incidence of sexual abuse among gay and lesbian individuals increased. Gradually, a view of a healthy sexuality and relationships emerged. However, the main focus was on preventing HIV infection not on developing emotionally healthy sexuality. In fact, some "safe" sexual practices developed that were not safe emotionally (circle jerks, telephone sex, Internet sex, pornography, etc.). Many thought that avoiding HIV infection was the main and only task in developing a healthy sexuality. The primary task in finding a partner who was compatible was limited to finding a partner who was sexually safe. Many men who were HIV infected were often left out of this discussion. Unfortunately, many continued in their promiscuous sexual behavior.

As many gay and bisexual HIV-negative men experienced the trauma of watching their friends and partners die from AIDS, they often became avoidant of sexuality and withdrew from others. Many did not have their intimacy and relationship needs met, and they adopted a perception that HIV infection was a part of being gay. Another misperception was the gay community's tendency to embrace AIDS as a political rather than a health issue. Some gay and bisexual men with AIDS were exalted as heroes in the gay community. The message of safe sex was obscured by this contradictory message. The many mixed messages about HIV and AIDS created a confusion that has hindered many men's attempts to develop healthy sexual and relationship behaviors.

Many gay and bisexual men simply gave up and abandoned any commitment to practice safe sex or seek a healthy relationship. Their depression and sense of helplessness indirectly led to self-destructive behavior through the abuse of substances and the practice of unsafe sex.

Support in the gay community for HIV-negative men has been very late in coming. The special needs of these men need to be recognized and nurtured. They deserve our praise and attention for developing healthy and lasting relationships despite the tremendous pressures of the last decade. They, too, are experiencing a great deal of loss and grief, as many of them survived the HIV/AIDS epidemic intact and healthy. Many men experience "survivors' guilt," and they have difficulty resolving their multiple losses.

The 1990s produced a movement in the gay community toward healthy sexuality and relationships. Gay and lesbian sexuality has been explored as a route to personal, physical, emotional, and spiritual growth. More and more, visibly committed couples are monogamous and sexually exclusive. A political movement is attempting to attain the legal right to be married or have a civil union. Couples are planning and having "holy unions" and celebrating their love for each other publicly. Many gay men and lesbians are seeking full parental, adoption, and foster care parental rights. Some would say that the gay community has arrived at full maturity. However, a decision to stop at this point would simply re-create the same problems of heterosexual couples who have had a very difficult time developing healthy marriages and families.

Gay, lesbian, and bisexual individuals have several strengths in regard to sexuality and relationships. They have the advantage of choosing to be spouses and parents, as there are no unplanned pregnancies and no societal pressures to marry as with heterosexuals. Gay men, bisexuals, and lesbians have the advantage of understanding sexuality from a profound sense of self-acceptance and appreciation.

The gay community and the broader society are experiencing a growing consciousness of the universal need of all people to love and be loved. This need is greater than the need for sexual freedom and multiple sexual partners. This type of love must develop fully to be complete. Many values that were traditionally associated with religion are now being adopted outside of the religious arena. These values include loyalty, selflessness, commitment, and a willingness to persist and endure in the face of difficulties. The gay community has embraced procreation as a value and many gay men, bisexuals, and lesbians are committing as joint partners in creating families. It has gained a wider perspective as an integral part of the overall society, and is no longer considered a particular side of downtown but has extended to the suburbs. Integration is evident in the broader society as gay men, bisexuals, and lesbians no longer hide their identities. They are celebrating their diversity as gays, bisexuals, and lesbians. A higher purpose exists as we enter this next millennium. Profound changes are occurring in our society as we move toward healing and community.

Those people involved in this movement are gaining awareness of a new truth. One new truth is that relationships can be happy and successful if individuals go through the proper preparation. An ideal person is out there for you, but you will not find him (or her) if you do not choose to go through your own personal growth and preparation. Your preparation sends a message to the universe that you are ready for a lasting relationship. Also, your ideal partner will not find you if he (or she) does not go through the same preparation. You will only continue to go through a series of failed relationships until this truth is revealed. Facing such a difficult challenge may seem insurmountable, but you have a great deal of support available to you at this time in history.

So here you are, embarking on this Great Adventure of preparing yourself. This book will not totally prepare you, but it will give you a guide for self-discovery and change that will result in a healthy relationship. The principles in this book are not unique and, in fact, have been used for generations. Creating a loving relationship may take several years, but you will be well on your way after reading this book. You will find the "right person" if you are simply willing to apply these principles and make the changes required for preparing yourself for your partner and soul mate.

PART I:
PREPARATION STAGE—
PREPARING YOURSELF
FOR A LASTING RELATIONSHIP

Chapter 1

Stop Running from Commitment

Life is difficult. This is a great truth, one of the greatest truths. It is a great truth because once we truly see this truth, we transcend it.

M. Scott Peck

Being gay and single is difficult. So little support exists for single people in general and even less support is evident for gay and bisexual men. Single people are often portrayed as failures or as inadequate: "If you were successful in finding a partner, you would not be single." The very word "single" conjures up images of desperation and loneliness. You may have shared the difficulties you are having with your married friends who placated you or told you that they only found their mate when they became perfectly content with being single. You may have attempted to find a lasting relationship and ended up believing you could only get sex. You may have decided that a celibate life is your only option and retreated into your solitary abode with a pint of ice cream to keep you company. Or you may have decided to pursue some misguided spiritual relationship as a means to fulfill all your longings rather than continue to look for a human relationship. (Not that there's anything wrong with spiritual relationships; they just can't touch you physically.) The truth is, you want a man!

However, you don't want just any man. You want a man who is capable of entering a healthy and lasting relationship. If you are like most single men, you have had your share of men who only wanted to have sex, men who were emotionally unavailable, men who were mentally inept, or men who were dependent and latched on to anyone who showed them attention. These experiences may have served to disillusion you and you may have come to believe that there are no healthy men available. You may have even "fallen in love" and risked yourself emotionally only to find that you had made an unhealthy decision or that you were unable to commit yourself. Whatever the reason, most single people have had numerous bad experiences and have had periods of wanting to give up. Fortunately, you have realized that you need more information and you have decided to read this book.

One thing you need to know is that likely nothing is wrong with you. Most people who have relationship or dating problems do not have the right skills to attract healthy partners and develop lasting relationships. Most people underestimate the efforts necessary to find a healthy partner. They often neglect developing the skills that do work. This book will show you how to develop those skills and the places where healthy men are found.

The first step is to make a commitment to finding a lasting relationship. This sounds easy, but it is actually somewhat difficult. Making a commitment means you must avoid detours such as seeking sexual relationships or hanging on to old relationships that are not working. Making a commitment means you must devote time, energy, and money to achieve your goal. You must make a commitment to being persistent even in the face of many obstacles. You must work to be consistent with your values, and you must resist the temptation to give in to easy sex. As a therapist and coach, I have seen the struggle individuals have when they set out to develop new behavioral patterns. There is a tendency to want "instant results." You have to avoid the urge to quit if the new behavior does not quickly produce results. Our society of fast-food and instant everything creates a basic impatience. Healthy dating skills and attaining your goal take diligence and persistence. You must pick yourself up after a bad experience and keep going if you want to achieve your goal.

Types of Relationships

1. *Nonexclusive dating relationship*—dating several partners with no commitment to any one of them.
2. *Exclusive dating relationship*—dating one partner exclusively with no long-term commitment.
3. *Cohabiting relationship*—living with a sexual or intimate partner; though there is an implied commitment, a cohabiting relationship does not always mean each partner is committed to each other; commitment needs to be verbalized and mutually agreed upon to be present in a relationship.

4. *Monogamous relationship*—a dating or committed relationship in which the partners agree to have no other sexual partners; monogamy and commitment are two separate entities though they are often thought to be synonymous.
5. *Committed/marital relationship*—a lasting and binding commitment which can be legal and permanent. Other terms for this type of relationship are domestic partnership or civil union. Many churches perform "holy unions" for same-sex couples.
6. *Open relationship*—a relationship in which one or both partners agree to have other sexual partners. The agreement is mutual, predetermined, and open among both parties. A strong commitment exists between the two main parties, though three or more individuals could join in an open relationship (e.g., polygamy).
7. *Sexual relationship*—a relationship that is primarily sexual and which does not involve any commitment. A sexual relationship can be very healthy if both parties agree on such a relationship and have open and honest communication.
8. *Friendship dating relationship*—a dating relationship in which there is no sexual involvement and which usually occurs when a couple is first dating. Friendship dating is certainly a lost art but it is vital in developing healthy dating relationships.

Any of these relationships can be very healthy. Most people think of a permanent relationship as one that is either monogamous or open and which involves some sort of commitment or joint purpose or goal (owning a house together, raising children together, etc.). A civil union is another term for a marital relationship that is legal in Vermont. Many other states are also moving toward legalization of civil unions and recognition of same-sex couples.

Intimacy with a partner is perhaps our most driving and most basic need. The desire to become one with another who can share your struggles and triumphs is the deepest need of all. The experience of gay and bisexual men hiding their sexuality in our society only serves to heighten their desperate struggle to meet this need. So much depends on how you face this challenge and yet so much is riding on the risk of failure. The power of this need is perhaps the reason so many men find themselves in bars, adult bookstores, or sex clubs seeking desperately to meet someone. Yet this route never really scratches the itch and they are off searching in vain again. A healthy connection may seem like an impossibility for you if you have already had many disappointing experiences. You may feel that the search is the only possibility for you as a gay or bisexual man, with no hope for creating a permanent relationship.

Let yourself fantasize for a moment. Not about the fantastic muscled stud you see as your pornographic dream man. Immerse yourself in a world of love, intimacy, and stability. Let go of all of your mistaken beliefs about what is and what is not possible for two men to have together. Let yourself ignore the religious bigots with all of their prejudice and homophobia and become surrounded by images of a home, a strong dependable man by your side, and a life of love together. This is your life if you can imagine it. You are not controlled by anything other than your own thoughts and dreams. Only your own beliefs and expectations limit you from finding the life you desire. Now set yourself in motion and get nearer to finding this dream. You are the master of your reality and you can have whatever you desire. You are only held back by your disbelief that you can have everything you want. Let go and allow yourself to enter this new world of possibility. You are now on your way.

Chapter 2

Have a Plan to Find Your Man

The men who build the future are those who know that greater things are yet to come, and that they themselves will help bring them about. Their minds are illumined by the blazing sun of hope. They never stop to doubt. They haven't time.

Melvin J. Evans

Okay, you finally decide to stop playing around with this dating and relationship thing and you decide to get serious. Once you have made a commitment, you will face another obstacle in your goal of finding a committed relationship. This barrier is overcoming the tendency to be too casual about dating. A misguided belief in our society is that finding a mate is spontaneous and that you can do nothing but wait until you find and meet that person. Think back to times when you did "fall in love at first sight," only to find out later that the person you thought was Mr. Wonderful was actually the worst possible choice. Careful planning and working toward your goal is a more realistic approach. You can keep this belief and wait until you meet the perfect person, or if you are tired of waiting, you may be ready for a fresh approach.

The myth of romantic love can allow us to be fooled into entering an unhealthy relationship and believe that we have only to find the "right person" to be happy. M. Scott Peck, in his book *The Road Less Traveled* (1978), discusses the tendency to fall prey to this misguided belief. He states that this belief will lead to a primary reliance on our feelings in choosing a partner. We may then believe we have made some terrible mistake when the initial passion wears off. We may begin to stray and break off the relationship to search for the "right one." We may become involved in an affair if we are partnered, as we seek to regain the feelings of falling in love again. We can make the mistake of believing that our task in finding a partner is to find this perfect person who will offer us perfect love and happiness. The only problem with this approach is that the feeling rarely lasts and we are left disillusioned and empty. Peck goes on to discuss that the task in finding a lasting relationship is self-growth and the letting go of immature and fantasy-based beliefs. He states that this is the same process that individuals who are in psychotherapy go through as they face their problems, let go of a fantasy-based understanding, and face the difficult and often painful reality.

If you want to achieve anything in life you must set a goal. You need to set your goal and work to achieve it within a specific time period. It may sound very strange to suggest you set a time period of finding your mate. Think about how you have achieved other goals. If you attended college and wanted to graduate, you set a date and planned your course schedule to complete the required courses in a specific time period. Having the time deadline made you more motivated and led to a clearer destination of your career. The same principle can be applied to finding a mate. People have a natural tendency to procrastinate and "put off until tomorrow what does not need to be done today." Dating too often gets put in the "put off until tomorrow" category, and days, weeks, and months go by with no efforts to meet new people and find a mate. A sense of hopelessness and powerlessness can then set in and lead to even more procrastinating and even dropping your goal.

Setting a specific and time-related goal may sound crazy. You may ask how you can control the outcome of finding a relationship given that this outcome depends on another person. The general rule is to set your goal between six and twelve months. You can always revise your target date if necessary. Setting a time limit will give you a sense of excitement and urgency you may not have at this time. Setting a target date may also allow you to get in touch with any fears or ambivalence you may have about being in a committed relationship. You may realize that you have been saying you wanted a committed relationship when at the same time you have resisted intimacy because of your fear of commitment. This issue will be developed in more detail in the next section on overcoming barriers to intimacy.

A specific outcome and date to achieve your goals allows you to focus and become motivated. Relationships do not simply happen. Setting a date will lead to daily and weekly goals to achieve the goal.

Breaking down a big task into smaller parts and working on each part in succession is another successful method for attaining your goal. I used this approach with my dissertation research when I was in graduate school. I was able to complete the project in two years with only a few hours each week devoted to the research itself. You will also allow yourself to be "in the process" rather than thinking you will not be successful until you find your partner. You will be going out and enjoying yourself and making many new friends. Getting out and doing something productive tends to lift the spirits. You will feel more optimistic about the goal you are seeking.

You are not going to find sheep in a cow pasture so you must get in the right place to find a relationship. A major step in finding your mate is going to the right places to meet healthy, available, relationship-oriented men. An impossible task you say! If you are like most, you have sought out potential dating partners in all the wrong places. The most unproductive place to meet healthy men is at bars. I am not opposed to bars and I am not judging the men who frequent bars. The fact is that many men go to gay bars to "cruise" for sex and nothing else. This type of person may say they are interested in dating simply to get what they want. Straight women know what I'm talking about.

I think that many gay men have bought into the idea that the gay community is synonymous with the bar scene and have limited their social contacts. A major problem with using bars to meet men is that you will also find a large percentage of men with alcohol and drug-abuse problems. The bars don't create these types of guys, but these guys tend to gravitate toward the bar scene. If you are going to include the bars as an outlet, just be direct with others. Say up front that you are looking for a potential partner and you are not interested in having a brief sexual encounter. This type of approach will repel those who are "cruising," and you will be free to meet healthy guys who are also seeking a committed relationship.

Places to Meet Available Dates Other Than Bars or Clubs

1. *Personal ads*
2. *Social groups*
3. *Church groups (circles)*
4. *Networking with friends*
5. *Volunteer work*
6. *Adult education classes*

7. *Singles groups*
8. *Clubs and activity-oriented groups*
9. *Dating services*
10. *Support groups*

Chapter 3

Face Your Fears of Getting Close

> It's obvious that many of the problems I have are the result of how things were when I was growing up. So here I am spending the rest of my life suffering for personality traits I never asked for. Where is the justice in that? But I was never promised justice.
>
> Hugh Prather

The biggest obstacle to overcome in your search to find a long-term partner is your own mind. Gay and bisexual men have been socialized in this homophobic society and many have accepted false beliefs about homosexuality. These false beliefs are largely unconscious and are similar to false beliefs and stereotypes about gender or racial differences. These beliefs are a powerful force in shaping your thoughts and behavior. However, you can make a conscious decision to identify your false beliefs and counter them with healthy beliefs. You may have adopted stereotypical views of being gay or bisexual and associated them with all gay or bisexual men. For example, you may believe that gay men are more creative and artistic than heterosexual men. You may believe that gay men are more sexually promiscuous than straight men and that gay men do not desire stable relationships. I saw this type of thinking occur recently when a well-known gay minister and his partner decided to adopt a child. A client of mine made the comment that the minister was attempting to appear "straight" by being partnered with children. He appeared to associate marriage and family with being "straight."

I am always amazed at how much the gay and bisexual men I have counseled put themselves down. I have seen this type of self-degradation in many of my clients and in myself. The phenomenon of internalizing negative beliefs by a minority group member is what I call "reverse stereotyping." Another term that has been used is "internalized homophobia," which refers to the unconscious adoption of negative beliefs about homosexuality or homosexuals by gay or bisexual men (see Forstein, 1988; Herek, 1984; Smith, 1988). These stereotypical beliefs are not based on facts, as the current psychological research has found no discernible personality differences between gay, bisexual, and heterosexual men (see Dean and Richardson, 1964; Miller, 1963; Ohlson and Wilson, 1974; Freedman, 1971; Saghir and Robins, 1973). These beliefs place limits on the individual, which is their major harm. For example, if I believe that gay men cannot be trusted, are sexually promiscuous, and do not have the ability to commit to a relationship, then I will expect a romantic partner to betray me and will actually choose unhealthy partners, as I will not perceive potential partners to be healthy. I may believe this about myself, adopt behaviors that reinforce my negative self-view, and convince myself I cannot be monogamous, thus giving up my goal of finding a committed partner. I may then give into a lifestyle of sexual permissiveness and forgo the goal of finding a meaningful and lasting relationship.

These are just a few mistaken beliefs I have heard from gay and bisexual clients as reasons they could not find a healthy partner. Many gay and bisexual men act out these stereotypical beliefs, as they do not know any other way to be gay or bisexual. They have given up any hope that a gay or bisexual life could be otherwise. Many of these men are disillusioned and jaded. This occurrence does not mean their beliefs are true.

This same type of reverse stereotyping is seen in other minorities. As a therapist, I have worked with African-American and Hispanic clients who believed they could not succeed in life because they were dark-skinned. They also thought that I could not understand their perception because I was light-skinned. Sexual orientation and skin color are not as powerful as they are made out to be in our society. Again, our beliefs about these attributes are the source of our limitations.

Mistaken Beliefs About Gay and Bisexual Men

Gay and bisexual men are

- sexually promiscuous
- not interested in a committed relationship

- only interested in sex
- materialistic and want only handsome and rich men
- incapable of monogamy and are not loyal sexually
- deceptive and dishonest
- always looking for a better-looking man and will leave you for him
- willing to take any sexual opportunity when it occurs
- not interested in having children
- all feminine and "nelly"
- not able to be Christian
- secretive about their sexual behaviors
- women haters
- preoccupied with youth and beauty
- only interested in the bar or "drag queen" scene
- infected with HIV and have AIDS
- neat and clean and obsessively organized
- not supportive of family values
- interested in "converting" other men to their lifestyle

[Add any other beliefs that come to your mind.]

- _____
- _____
- _____

Don't get me wrong: prejudice does exist, but much of the perceived prejudice is self-generated. You perceive that you are a victim and look for those who hate you or who want to limit you. Your own aggressive behavior then acts to reinforce your victim role. Southern Baptists are often seen as persecutors of gays and bisexuals, something I have heard over and over. In reality, there are fewer Southern Baptists than there are gay and bisexual men, yet the victim mentality continues. Even if Southern Baptists were a real threat, they are only one segment of one denomination of one religion in our society. They hardly represent a threat, except to themselves. You are usually your own greatest enemy. Hate begets hate and you soon become the very thing you despise.

Another barrier for many gay and bisexual men is their general lack of emotional and social development. Most have not had the opportunity to explore their sexuality. They have not been allowed to develop dating and intimate relationships from adolescence, as have their heterosexual counterparts. Many gay and bisexual men feel alienated from all men due to their fear of rejection and their own homophobia. They may have many adolescent notions of sexuality and may be emotionally unprepared for the demands of an intimate relationship. In *Identity: Youth and Crisis* (1968), Eric Erikson discussed the developmental stages that affect the adolescent's development of an identity and capacity to enter into an intimate relationship. He developed a stage model of development and discussed the tasks of identity formation and the capacity for intimacy.

The development of identity occurs in adolescence and the successful resolution of this stage is required before an individual can develop the capacity for intimacy. Erikson stated that the development of an identity is composed of a sexual identity, morals and values, career and life choices, an identification with the community and society. He added that the damaging effects of a nonsupportive social environment often derail the resolution of a masculine identity. He emphasized that this process is highly dependent on the influence of parents, families, peers, churches, communities, and society in general. Most gay and bisexual youth do not receive the support necessary to successfully develop a clear and stable sense of themselves as healthy and accepting men.

Barriers to Intimacy
(The Three B's)

The following three areas are usually the main barriers to developing an intimate relationship. Please take some time to consider if an aspect of your intimate relationships could be affected by any one of these areas. Write down in those areas that may be a barrier to developing an intimate relationship.

Beliefs. What are your beliefs about other men and relationships? List your negative beliefs about same-sex relationships and intimacy that could be blocking you:

_____

_____

_____

_____

Baggage. What learning experiences in your family background could be impairing your ability to form an intimate relationship? What areas of dysfunction did you inherit?

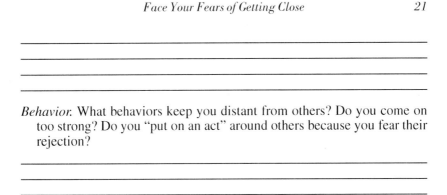

Behavior. What behaviors keep you distant from others? Do you come on too strong? Do you "put on an act" around others because you fear their rejection?

The result of this delayed development is being stuck in an adolescent mode of relating to oneself and others. Sexual and relationship behaviors of gay and bisexual men often reflect this immaturity. There is often an overemphasis on the physical aspects of a partner and an excessive focus on physical appearance and superficial traits such as success and money. Many men convince themselves that attaining these surface traits in a partner will somehow convey social status and importance. Gay and bisexual men also act impulsively and make poor choices. Often excessive sexual experimentation occurs in an attempt to make up for lost time. Unsafe sex is an expression of this impulsivity. Many men become overwhelmed when a relationship becomes intimate and they feel trapped and closed in. These are all characteristics commonly found in adolescents.

This immaturity may cause you to repeat the same pattern again and again. You may come to believe that this is "normal." You may also see this behavior in others and convince yourself you are just doing what other gay and bisexual men are doing. The danger of settling into this type of sexuality is that you never grow up and you remain an adolescent in your relationship functioning. You need to identify the immature and impulsive behaviors that keep you from developing a close and lasting relationship before you can develop a lasting partnership.

Chapter 4

Don't Try to Succeed Alone

> Your friend is your needs answered. He is your field which you sow with love and reap with thanksgiving. And he is your board and your fireside. For you come to him with your hunger, and you seek him for peace.
>
> Kahlil Gibran

It is difficult to succeed at any task alone. A successful dating program will depend on the support of many people. You will need a support system if you are going to find a compatible partner. Many single people have either dated one person or been isolated, and they have not developed a broad basis of social support.

A member of my support system connected me with my partner. I met my partner at church, but it was not during a church service. I was a friend of one of the church staff members and I was working at the church's counseling center. My future partner had come to a "Bach lunch," a musical organ service accompanied by lunch, served at the church. He saw me while he was eating with our mutual friend. This friend had listened to me tell of my struggles with dating and my desire to find a partner. He encouraged my future partner to introduce himself. I was not sure what was happening at the time. I soon figured out that he was interested in a date and we set one up. If I had not included our mutual friend in my support system, this opportunity may have been missed.

To get people to support you, you must let them know that you are looking for a partner. The prospect of presenting yourself as available and open to the scrutiny of others in a dating or singles situation is frightening for most men. This approach often conjures up images of being displayed to others as in a singles bar or appearing desperate. This fear will keep you from presenting yourself as available if you allow it. You have to overcome these fears and remember that you are not only "selling" yourself to prospective partners, but that you are also "shopping" for a compatible mate. If you were looking for a used car, you would probably look in as many places you could think of until you found the right buy. You would probably ask all of your friends if they knew of a used car for sale and you would "advertise" your need. This same principle works for finding a mate.

Your friends can be incredibly good resources, as they already know you and your tastes and interests. They have social connections you do not have and they essentially "double your efforts." Always be ready to accept an invitation to a party or an offer for a blind date from a friend. If you refuse the offer you may not get any other invitations. Also, do not chastise your friend if a blind date does not work out. You will embarrass and insult him or her and you will lose their support and possibly their friendship. Always thank a friend for assisting you and accept the awkwardness if the situation does not work out. Your friends may fix you up with another blind date that is the man of your dreams.

Much support exists for sexual activity in the gay community. Sex may seem easy and dating often appears elusive and uncommon. You may not know where to go to develop a support system. A dating workshop such as the one I conduct can be an excellent resource. I call my dating workshops "Finding a Lover for Life," and I have conducted them for the past seven years with a very good response and attendance. Dating workshops are often given in churches or counseling centers and they are an excellent way to meet other single men who are dealing with the same issues. You may not meet your mate at a workshop, but you may make friends who can be part of your dating support system. Many men are embarrassed to admit they have had difficulty in finding a mate. This shame dates back to the socialization most men receive. In our society, men are supposed to be "studs" and never have a problem finding sex and affection, right? Beliefs such as this one often keep men from seeking out valuable resources.

Another major issue for gay and bisexual men is developing friendships with other gay and bisexual men. Being close to other gay men without having sex with them is difficult for most. You need to develop a large social network of other gay and bisexual men in order to meet many single men. Many men do not know how to develop this type of social network as they have been used to being "closeted" toward other men. Being in a large group of other men may feel awkward or scary. You may be used to the "cruising" style of interacting with other men. Some settings tend to sexualize other men and this type of situation is very intimidating. You may fear rejection and this may cause you to isolate yourelf, You can do this, or you can say, "If you can't beat them, then join them." You may then adopt the cruising attitudes of other men and interact in this same manner.

Developing a healthy social network is a difficult task. You will need to seek out men with similar values and interests. Many non-bar social groups for gay and bisexual men allow healthy ways to interact with other men. Some groups are mixed with men and women and this kind of mix can also be very beneficial. Many lesbians have single gay male friends and they can act as great matchmakers. Many churches are welcoming of gay and bisexual attendants and offer single groups and social functions. In these types of settings, you learn to let down your guard and develop skills in genuinely interacting with others. Support groups can also be helpful in developing dating and social skills. General therapy groups can help develop social skills. The main point to remember is your goal of finding a mate. You need to have a large pool of potential dating partners to pull from if you are going to find someone with whom you are compatible. If you simply "let it happen," you may not find the right person. Having a large social network to draw upon will allow you to meet many men and also have a fun time while you are meeting them. Many social activities can be rewarding even if you do not gain a date or meeting from them. Some social settings will remain in your social network after you find a mate and this continued support will also be necessary to maintain a healthy and stable relationship. In many ways, you will be developing the skills you need to be in a relationship while you are single. Men in relationships need the support of others to deal with the stresses and problems unique to partnered life.

Friends who are in relationships can also be a great resource. One of my goals when I was single was to learn how my partnered friends were maintaining a successful relationship. I often went to social gatherings with individuals in relationships and observed their interactions and conversations. I learned a great deal about how successful couples interacted. This learning process was very important for me, as I had no role models of successful same-sex relationships. I also attended a presentation by a gay man who had been partnered for over fifty years. I remember how astounded I was as I listened to a man who had attained my dream. Gradually, I began to believe that I could attain a lasting and healthy relationship. I also gained a great deal of knowledge listening to them share about the dynamics of partnered life. They were and still are a valuable source of information for me. My partner and I attend a male couples' Bible study group and the sharing in this group has been invaluable.

Close friends can also be a very good source of feedback though this feedback may be difficult to hear. I made very little progress when I called my friends for "sympathy" after several bad dating experiences. I began making progress when I decided to take their advice. One friend told me, "Why do you wait to be dumped by these men? If you sense that things are not working out, you can take the initiative and end the relationship. The way you are doing it, you are always getting hurt and feeling like a victim!" This feedback was not easy to hear, but it was a major tuning point in how I related to men in a dating situation.

I remember that at one point in my dating I decided to try everything my friends had suggested and I stopped discounting their suggestions. Some of their recommendations seemed odd but I decided to keep an open mind and try new things, as the things I had been doing were not working. This attitude of open-mindedness is very important if you want to succeed at any new task. You may have found yourself discounting suggestions in this book. Such a stance is very self-defeating. You will need to try different ways of doing things if you want to succeed. Keep an open mind and you will have an open heart.

A support network can keep you going when you get discouraged and you want to isolate or give into old patterns. While dating, there will be many times that you will become discouraged. You will have "dry periods" in which you may not have any dates or meetings planned. During these "low" periods, friends can offer you support, encouragement, and affection that will allow you to continue in your search. Professional support groups exist for people who are unemployed and seeking another job, and I have had many clients attend these groups. They work as they offer the participants support and encouragement to continue a difficult task. Your own support network of friends can work in the same manner and can prevent the temptation to give into despair. Their support will also keep you from wasting time by isolating or "giving up." Other single people who are staying positive about finding a partner can also offer you valuable support. You will become part of their support system and will live out the positive attitudes you find yourself saying to them when they are discouraged or despondent.

Your social network can also be part of making being single and dating "fun." You will give up many things when you finally find a partner and you may want to enjoy your single life while you still have the time. Your social group could be composed of others who have similar interests and hobbies. Hundreds of such groups exist, largely composed of single men and women. You will need to have fun while you are dating or you will give it up entirely.

When you are interacting in a social group where the focus is not "cruising," your best qualities are likely to emerge. You will not be focused on whether you have a date and you will feel more relaxed and freer to interact with other single men. This kind of social group will allow you to develop social skills in interacting with other men in a nonsexual manner. The end result of your participation in such a group will be greatly improved social skills and recreation, which are pluses even if you do not find a dating partner in that particular group.

Chapter 5

Prepare Yourself Emotionally

A man cannot possibly be at peace with others until he has learned to be at peace with himself.

Bertrand Russell

Now that you have decided to take the plunge into the icy waters of healthy dating, you open yourself to many new and uncomfortable feelings. Dating is an emotional experience, and no amount of rational thinking will alter the effects of your past family experiences and background. Many men do not realize the internal barriers they create to healthy dating. These are usually unique to each individual, but some of them are worth discussing. One major barrier is unresolved hurt and rejection from a parental figure. In *Being Homosexual* (1989), Richad Isay explored his perception that many gay and bisexual men have been rejected by their fathers and have had close relationships with their mothers. He discussed this paternal rejection in terms of the damage that occurs in establishing an identity as a boy and man when difficulty bonding with the father occurs. He stated that the relationship with the same-sex parent was the most important relationship in forming introjects for later same-sex relationships. If this bonding did not occur or was conflictual, then problems with bonding in an adult relationship occur. While this theory may not be true of all gay and bisexual men, this dynamic is common for many.

Most gay and bisexual men have been traumatized in their childhood from prejudice about their sexual orientation. These men feel rejected from fathers and brothers who are unable to accept their sexuality. Their homophobia is highly socialized, as much of what is connected to homosexuality in our society is associated with being unmasculine and unmanly. Also, a father may be unable to affirm his son's masculinity if he has not been able to resolve his own homophobia. Some fathers are gay or bisexual themselves but they have suppressed their own homosexual impulses. These fathers apply this same rigidity to their sons. Some fathers are verbally abusive and they taunt their sons in the "hopes" of eliminating any signs of their own homosexuality. Some men who are gay or bisexual have feminine traits and they may have been rejected because of them.

A personal experience comes to mind. I wanted to play the piano when I was nine and when I asked my father, I clearly remember him saying, "Only women or faggots play the piano." I did not know what he meant at the time and I shared his reaction with my mother. She was enraged and made sure I received piano lessons and my own piano. This memory was etched in my mind long before I realized and accepted that I was gay. I remember that my father hated to hear my piano practice and he had to be dragged to recitals. However, the damage was done and I was sure I was not the son my father had wanted. My brother played football and I remember the excessive attention he received. We all attended his games as a family and almost never missed them. The message I received is that football was okay and piano was not.

Richard Isay describes paternal rejection as gay and bisexual men not receiving the affirmation and acceptance of their fathers. This acceptance is essential in the development of a sound masculine identity and in the awareness of other men as emotionally safe. Paternal rejection keeps gay and bisexual men from feeling safe and they learn to emotionally distance themselves from other men. They reenact this sense of rejection and lack of affirmation through superficial sex, an easy and familiar way to interact with other men when intimacy is uncomfortable and foreign.

Some gay and bisexual men may give up trying to be masculine. They identify with their mothers and assume feminine mannerisms. Don't get me wrong. I know there are some men who are truly more feminine than masculine, and there is nothing wrong with this type of personality style. However, many men have never been comfortable with their masculinity and have not developed this aspect of their personality. Some men overcompensate for a sense of inadequacy and become overly masculine or "butch." They reject any femininity in themselves in much the same manner their fathers rejected the femininity they perceived. Anna Freud (1936) called this dynamic "identification with the aggressor," in which the victim of abuse assumes the traits of the perpetrator in an attempt to feel in control of the abusive situation. In this way, gay and bisexual men continue to persecute themselves and intensify their feelings of rejection and low self-worth.

Internalized rejection and homophobia can carry over to relationships with other men, resulting in a lack of trust or fear of rejection. Some men who were unable to hide their homosexuality experienced intense rejection from other boys and adult men (e.g., teachers and coaches). I have counseled gay men who experienced "deprogramming" attempts from misguided ministers and parents.

Some men bring this shame and rejection into therapy and support groups in which the focus is to "eliminate" their homosexuality. When the person finally gains the courage to "come out" as gay or bisexual, the same patterns of rejection are often repeated over and over with other gay and bisexual men.

There are other relationship patterns related to rejection from a father. A gay man may become very rejecting of his own femininity and hate feminine or "nelly" men. A gay or bisexual man may marry a woman and seek out secretive sexual relations with other men. A gay man may appear to always be in control and seek out only the most handsome and masculine partners in an attempt to feel validated. A gay man may be critical of some gay men and prize his "social standing" in the gay community as a way of receiving the attention he did not receive from his father. An individual may long for closeness, but may fear harm from another and may pull away when the relationship gets too close. Another individual may find it is safer to give in to a pattern of sexual promiscuity and rejection of his partners. These are only a few of the destructive relationship patterns I have observed in my clients. The good news is you can overcome these destructive patterns, learn from past experiences, and develop a healthy self-image.

Gay and bisexual men experience other emotional barriers to intimacy as a result of rejection or abandonment by either parent. Lack of appropriate role models and family disruption can also impede a child's developing sense of trust and security. Growing up in an addictive family can cause severe trust and intimacy problems. The addiction can be alcohol, drugs, food, sex, money, work, or religion. Any of these can preoccupy the adult caregivers' attention and children are emotionally neglected. Physical, sexual, or verbal abuse of any kind also prevent the child from developing healthy relationship skills. Some men grow up attempting to "help" and rescue a dysfunctional parent and repeat this pattern over and over again in relationships with an addicted or dysfunctional partner. Some men develop an addiction themselves and seek to be taken care of or rescued by others, but their addiction may only push others away and they are often left alone and unhappy. Another pattern is to become overly vigilant for any sign that the relationship is not working. The "relationship phobic" person runs at the slightest sign of trouble, believing that they are avoiding harm. The harm is always perceived as real and any attempt to convince them that they are acting irrationally fails.

Many gay and bisexual men do not feel worthy of a successful relationship. They have internalized so many negative messages about themselves that they sabotage their own success. The story of Cinderella is applicable to the experience many men have of not feeling worthy. As you recall, Cinderella was treated very badly by her stepmother and was forced to serve her two stepsisters. She was told that her sisters were worthy of love and attention from others, but that she was not worthy of such love. The reason for this treatment had nothing to do with Cinderella and was her stepmother's issue. However, Cinderella came to believe she could never find true love. She longed for her Prince Charming who would take her away from all of her problems. What gay man cannot relate to her fantasy! However, when she was granted her wish by her fairy godmother and she went to the ball and met her Prince she did not feel worthy of his love. She ran away, leaving only her shoe as identification. Even when the Prince found her with her shoe, she sought to hide, as she felt unworthy of his love.

Cinderella's story rings true for many who have struggled with negative messages about themselves. Gay and bisexual men can overcome this pattern and recognize the tendency to self-sabotage themselves. The fairy godmother in the Cinderella story represents the spiritual self that can be a resource in self-healing. You can learn to believe in yourself and see yourself as worthy and beautiful as a gay or bisexual man. You can learn to overcome the barriers of self-doubt and self-consciousness that have kept you from stepping out and developing healthy relationships. You can also allow yourself to feel worthy of another's love and affection once you find a healthy partner. The Cinderella Complex does not need to defeat you. Overcome your fears and allow the good things in life to happen to you.

Many self-defeating patterns will likely require therapy to resolve. You may have repeated these patterns so often that you feel helpless to change them. Harvel Hendrix, in his book *Getting the Love You Want* (1988), addressed the destructive patterns that develop in our parental relationships. Identifying them is the most important step in changing these patterns. If you can identify them, you can at least make a goal of avoiding the behaviors related to your patterns. You can then work to develop healthy attitudes and behaviors that will allow you to get close to other men. Letting go of the old hurt, pain, and anger is a goal you can work on in therapy. Letting go of these trapped feelings will allow you to experience a freedom you may have never known. I remember very clearly the day I realized I was no longer lonely all the time and that I could love and approve of myself regardless of the fact that my father did not know how to love me. I realized I was not my father's child and was no longer controlled by him. His rejection of me was his problem and was no longer mine. What freedom I experienced when I realized this truth!

Sexual abuse can be particularly damaging to an individual's ability to form healthy relationships. Many men did not realize they were being sexually abused as minors. Similar to heterosexual boys who are sexual with adult females, they may perceive that they were "lucky." They may have come to believe that these early sexual experiences actually allowed them to accept their sexuality and feel affirmed. What they do not realize is that this type of sexual abuse teaches the victim many inappropriate lessons about sex. Abuse teaches that sex is impersonal, that sex can be separate from an emotional connection, that sex should be secret or that any sexual expression is okay as long as "both parties are willing." These experiences become significant in the formation of a sexual identity as the younger person grows up. These sexual behaviors and attitudes may be repeated and the individual may wonder why intimacy is never attained. Many men who were sexually abused also develop sexual addiction or compulsivity. They may engage in anonymous, risky, or illegal sexual behaviors and may have poor boundaries in their relationships.

Another major barrier I have seen in my clients is disillusionment with ever finding a lasting relationship. Unfortunately, many gay and bisexual men believe the stereotypes of homosexuality and doubt they can ever attain monogamous and lasting relationships. Some

may even claim that a monogamous relationship is based on a heterosexual model of relationships and that gay and bisexual men are free
from these types of restraints. Nothing is wrong with being single and
having many sexual partners. However, this is not true for all gay or
bisexual men.

Written statements about gay and bisexual men being free from the
responsibilities of relationships, marriage, and family have come
back to haunt the gay community. The recent debate over same-sex
marriage displayed the gay community's horribly inadequate preparation for this debate. Little evidence exists of gay men and bisexuals
seeking and maintaining lasting and monogamous relationships and
many have used this lack of finding as a reason to abandon this goal.
Beware of the temptation to "just go along with society." To develop
your own set of values and choices, you need to seek out your own
personal goals and forget about what "society" says you should do or be.

I find it amazing that we claim to be so proudly nonconforming as
gay and bisexual men, yet we become timid about our own values and
beliefs once we come out. I have been criticized for my conservative
values and beliefs, and I do not relate to most of what people call the
"gay lifestyle." I remained "closeted" for so long because I thought I
would have to be promiscuous and socialize at bars if I were out-
wardly gay. Fortunately, I found a gay and lesbian church, Metropoli-
tan Community Church, in Dallas, Texas. There I met men and
women who shared my conservative beliefs and values, and who
were neither pulled by the society at large or the "gay community" in
deciding who they were and what they were about. They were truly
"their own people," and they did not give in to social pressures. My
partner and I committed to one another in this church. Perhaps this
type of experience may also allow you to realize your goals and create a healthy support system.

Having positive values will not be easy if you are gay and bisexual
and many will oppose you, even from within our own "community."
The community of gay and bisexual individuals is actually incredibly
diverse and there is no one proper type. We may choose to unite for
political reasons, but we do not have to buy into the many generaliza-
tions we make about ourselves.

You may have tried very hard to find a relationship only to discover
that many gay and bisexual men are caught up in this very social pressure. They may be afraid to "come out" and avoid socializing with

gay and bisexual men altogether. They may adopt all of the "gay trap-pings" and socialize in bars and dress in drag on Halloween. They may swish and display nelly traits that they associate as gay manner-isms. They may seek to be the most attractive, work out for two hours every day, and drive a Porsche. They may cheat on their boyfriend and may use their fear of intimacy as an excuse to break off poten-tially healthy relationships. You may meet men who are so disillu-sioned that they simply grab sex wherever it happens and avoid the possibility of a dating situation. All of these possibilities may occur when you begin dating, and you may have even adopted several of these patterns yourself. For many, the end result of these patterns is disillusionment and despair.

I see this despair every day as I counsel gay and bisexual men. I am very confrontive of these dysfunctional patterns of coping with being gay. I do not believe being gay or bisexual is a disorder, but many of the ways we think we have to be "gay" do cause much of our confu-sion. Be yourself and avoid trying to conform and "fit into" any mold, gay or straight. The true "political" movement of gay and bisexual men will be when we liberate ourselves from needing to conform to these patterns and assert who we are in society. We will likely look and act just like everyone else and there will be no reason to "fear" us. This does not mean we simply assimilate, but it means we allow our-selves to be ourselves and to be a part of society. We err when we iso-late ourselves in a heterophobic manner and see ourselves as "differ-ent." We are all very similar in this human condition and there are more similarities than differences. This similarity crosses all barriers, gender, race, sexual orientation, age, financial status, profession, or ethnicity. Eventually we will see others' similarities, but we must first appreciate and value our own diversity.

The real danger of not recognizing these patterns is that they can sabotage success in our dating relationships. These patterns may be related to growing up in a dysfunctional family, being rejected by our fathers, failing to resolve our own internalized homophobia, or as-suming the socialized attitudes of many in our own community. When you recognize these patterns in your own sexual and relation-ship behaviors, you are then able to change. The first and most impor-tant step is that you are totally honest with yourself about being in this pattern. You may be surprised to discover that many of these patterns are very strange and based on beliefs to which you are firmly committed. You may have to work very hard to allow yourself to develop new beliefs. However, this hard work will be rewarded, not only in being happier, but also in finding a lasting and healthy relationship.

The following is a list of fifteen "sabotage patterns" I have identified in gay and bisexual men. Can you identify your particular patterns?

1. *The Perfect Lover.* This pattern is related to the "halo effect," which occurs when we find someone physically attractive. We tend to associate many other positive qualities to this person and may miss their faults and problems. This pattern is also related to the misguided belief that physical attraction equals love. Individuals who are looking for their "prince" or "princess" may also believe that once they find this "true connection," there will be no problems and all will be wonderful. However, they risk missing a potentially good relationship once the glow wears off.

2. *I'll play it safe so I won't get hurt again.* This pattern occurs when we have been hurt in past relationships and become guarded in future dating experiences to avoid another painful experience. This pattern can lead to totally closing off healthy partners. Individuals build walls and will only let them down when totally sure the other person will not hurt or abandon them. As a result, many dating partners give up trying to get close and go away, and this subsequent rejection only serves to confirm their belief in abandonment.

3. *All I need is love.* This pattern is characteristic of those who are love and romance addicted. They seek out a relationship as a means of escaping the mundane worldly plane and transcend into a perfect world of romance and love, free from all worry and pain. These individuals tend to fall in love with a fantasy rather than a real person and forever search for the "right person" to fall in love with.

4. *I say yes when I want to say no.* This pattern is common in individuals who have poor sexual boundaries and who become sexual too quickly with a dating partner. The level of emotional intimacy does not match the level of sexual involvement and they often become uncomfortable when the other person wants a closer relationship. They have the tendency to focus on the other person as the source of the relationship failure and do not perceive their own poor sexual boundaries that led to difficulty establishing emotional intimacy.

5. *It's not possible, so why try?* These individuals have had several failures at establishing a committed relationship and they come to be-

lieve they cannot be faithful to a partner. They may have entered relationships with the hope of having an "open relationship," or thought that they could be liberal and share their partner sexually only to learn that they had sacrificed their true values and happiness with these beliefs. As a result, they often become disillusioned and jaded about the possibility of establishing monogamy in a relationship.

6. *I can't let you really know me.* This pattern is often seen in individuals who have low self-esteem and who do not believe they are worthy of another person's love. They often have a family background of rejection or abandonment and may feel that others will also reject them. They may yearn for a loving relationship only to sabotage one when it does occur. They may also seek out unhealthy partners as they do not feel deserving of a healthy partner.

7. *I can't ever get enough sex.* This pattern is seen in those who are sexually addicted or who have been sexually abused. They have learned to meet their emotional needs by being sexual and have few skills in meeting their intimacy needs. They confuse passion with love and closeness yet only achieve "pseudo-intimacy." Their relationships are usually short-lived, yet exciting, which leads them to pursue another sexual relationship when they encounter problems.

8. *I can be whoever you want.* These individuals are codependent personalities and tend to conform themselves to their partner's desires, in a vain attempt to "win" undying love. They tend to attract dominant personalities who control them. If they have attracted a healthy partner, their partner becomes bored and the relationship fizzles. The codependent person then feels unloved and abandoned and may feel hopeless about dating and relationships.

9. *Are you going to leave me too?* This pattern is seen in individuals who have been abandoned in their childhood and who have come to expect rejection in their relationships. They tend to focus on the slightest signs of rejection (e.g., an unreturned phone call, a canceled date, etc.) as a sign they are being rejected and may actually reject the other person first as a means to "protect" themselves. The result is that they sabotage even healthy relationships and feel rejected and despondent.

10. *I only know how to compete.* This pattern is seen in individuals who are competitive and dominant and who are more comfortable initiating than receiving. They fail to recognize the need for others to also initiate affection and they may alienate others' desire to care for

them. They may also compete to be "the best" with their partner, who may cause the other person to withdraw and pull away from the relationship.

11. *I can't let you get too close.* These individuals tend to project fears of being hurt onto others and perceive they will be hurt if they allow others to get too close. They tend to have "walls," which protect them and will not allow others to harm or love them. However, these walls usually work too well and end up keeping potential partners away.

12. *The hunt is more fun than the catch.* This pattern is seen in individuals who are addicted to the thrill of finding a new romance and "catching" their prize. They go from person to person in the hope of finding something lasting, but the thrill quickly wears off and they are left feeling empty and confused. They are then off to another chase and all is forgotten.

13. *I need you to need me.* This pattern is similar to the codependent pattern and these individuals tend to enter a relationship as a "caregiver" or "rescuer." They hope to win their partner's affection by being overly generous. They may be initially received for their generosity that is later rejected as smothering or controlling. Their partners may also resent the inequality in this type of relationship and may pull back in an attempt to regain their sense of independence.

14. *You can't trust other men.* These individuals may have been hurt in past relationships and may have difficulty trusting. However, they generalize their fears to all dating partners and do not allow themselves to take risks. There is no guarantee any of us will not be hurt in life, but these individuals seek total security in a relationship and they never find it.

15. *I'm always attracted to the wrong person.* These individuals have few skills in finding someone who is compatible with them and they end up with unhealthy partners. When their relationships do not work, they assume that all relationships are doomed to fail. They do not realize that they may need to develop better skills in finding a compatible mate. They may also fail to realize the need to hold off "falling in love," and date long enough to find out if the person is truly compatible.

Chapter 6

Let Go of Old Entanglements

Don't hang on to anger, hurt or pain. They steal your energy and keep you from love.

Leo Buscaglia

You may believe that any relationship is better than no relationship, but nothing could be further from the truth. Many people settle for any available partner and they believe they cannot attract a better one. Some men hang on out of fear that prevents them from being available to an appropriate partner. Other men engage in affairs or cheat on a partner in a misguided attempt to resolve their confusion. These self-destructive behaviors only keep these men from developing healthy relationships. You do not have to be one of these men. You can choose to let go of unhealthy relationships, no matter how difficult.

A common mistake made by many men is to hang on to a partner long after the relationship has ended. In order to make room for a healthy relationship, you need to let go of all attachments to old boyfriends. Pictures and gifts given by ex-boyfriends displayed around your home signal your unwillingness to be open to a new partner. You need to make room for the new person that will be your partner. The decision to let go of your old attachments and memories is difficult, but necessary. As soon as you release your attachments, you will realize that they have kept you stuck in the past and have not allowed you to move on with your life. A helpful way of letting go is to find a ritual that will assist you symbolically in letting go. You can melt down an old ring and make a new one, you can sell old gifts and clothes given to you by an old boyfriend, or you can throw away old pictures and cards. A ritual that will allow you to grieve and release your past partners will be very liberating!

You need to create a "vacuum" of a healthy self with no unhealthy attachments in order to attract a healthy partner. Your goal is to prepare a place in your heart and life for your partner. Preparing for your mate may mean you will be lonely and anxious at times, but it will also mean you will be available. Availability is the most important quality in attracting a mate. If you are involved in another relationship or having casual sex, you will not be available when healthy dating partners appear. Being available is different from being needy and dependent. You will still benefit from going slow when you find a healthy partner.

You will also have a great deal of time alone during your dating project. This alone time can be an opportunity to develop yourself and your interests. You will need to avoid the temptation to fill up your emptiness with being with someone. The experience of tolerating frustration and loneliness is very important. If you become impatient and grab on to the nearest dating partner, you may miss your opportunity to connect with the right person. Available men will avoid you if they think you are in a relationship. They do not know that you are ready to leave the person you are currently dating. If you are honest with yourself, you will be able to admit how unhealthy hanging on to an unhealthy relationship is for you. Let go and allow yourself to feel your pain and aloneness and make this a comfortable state of being, not one you wish to avoid by seeking out someone.

Why is having casual sex while you are attempting healthy dating so counterproductive? Why do you need to avoid the temptation to latch on to a sexual relationship out of your own sexual frustration? Promiscuous sexual behavior can backfire and you can gain a reputation as "easy." You will then find that you are getting lots of attention from the wrong types of guys. Unfortunately, many gay and bisexual men view these types of interactions as healthy. This type of promiscuous sexuality may have been modeled to you. Movies and television also portray promiscuity as normal sexual and dating behavior. Unhealthy sexual behavior repels potential healthy partners and you will continue to be frustrated and disappointed. You will need to be a person with relationship values if you want to attract a man with relationship values. You may end up in a relationship with promiscuous sexual behavior and attain a partner who cheats on you or who wants to have multiple sexual partners. You are who you attract. Start being the person you want to attract now.

Many gay and bisexual men feel very lonely because of their history of isolation from other men. You may have difficulty getting out of a relationship that is not working because you fear loneliness. Staying in a relationship to avoid being lonely is the worst reason for a relationship. You can be very lonely in a bad relationship, and your unwillingness to face this is actually your unwillingness to grow emotionally.

Facing your loneliness will be difficult but you will grow emotionally and become mature and independent as a result. You may need to seek out a therapist to assist you in understanding the source of your loneliness and your negative reactions to being alone. You may have never let go of your early childhood dependency on your parents. You may have been emotionally abandoned or neglected as a child and you may be unconsciously seeking to replace you primary attachments. Your decision to get out of a relationship that is not working may bring up intense pain. You will need to face your feelings if you want to attract a healthy partner. An immature, underdeveloped individual will attract the same type of individual. This issue may actually be the core issue of your inability to find a healthy partner.

Alternately, you may realize that the person you are committed to is not the right person for you. Such a realization can be very distressing. Most people do not realize how complicated life becomes when you make a decision to live with a partner until they need to get out of a relationship that is not working. Holding off on living with a partner is very sound advice, though many have made the mistake of living with someone prematurely. Gay and bisexual men are especially prone to live together without a commitment because there is no legal or social support involved. A sound general rule is to only live with someone you are committed to and who you are sure is a compatible choice. The temptation to set up a household with a person because your sexual relationship is good, you are lonely, or because of finances or convenience are all recipes for disaster.

Chapter 7

Make Room for a Relationship

There is a time to let things happen and a time to make things happen.

Hugh Prather

I am always amazed at the amount of energy, time, and money people spend on their careers, houses, cars, or vacations, yet they resist the suggestion of investing time, money, and energy in finding a partner. Many people view dating as a mystical and spontaneous process that happens beyond one's control. They view relationships as part of "destiny" to which they must passively submit. You may have also developed such idealized beliefs about relationships. The downside of these beliefs is that you may give up looking for a partner and come to believe that you were destined not to have a relationship. You may resign to fate and become depressed and isolated. You may also give in to just having sex or dating a temporary lover and resign yourself to accept your fate.

Anything worth having is worth planning and working for. You may wonder how you can plan your dating so you can attain a relationship. Focus on three basic issues: time, money, and energy. Your first goal in finding a partner is to commit time in your schedule for socializing and meeting available men. You may have used being too busy or working too much in the past to avoid facing the issue of dating. This avoidance mechanism has worked for you and it will be difficult to change. You may have decided that you would focus on your career and work since you did not have anyone to come home to. You may be working entirely too much. The downside is that your overworking has likely led to career and financial success. You may find it difficult to let go of any extra work time. This transition will be a major decision point for you as you now face your priorities. Either finding a partner is your first priority or being a success at work is your first priority. You will probably make less money and you may not be president of your company before you are thirty, but you will not be alone at night if you decide to make time for dating.

You may also decide to spend less time with friends and other leisure activities. Remember that you have to invest time to meet a variety of men if you are going to find a compatible mate. You may be able to combine some activities, but your main focus needs to be meeting available men in multiple social settings. You may see this type of focus as being desperate or as "cruising." Nothing could be farther from the truth. You are merely focusing on your goal of connecting with available men in order to find possible dating partners.

The second goal in finding a mate is investing money in your search. I am amazed at how much money people will spend on going out and drinking and on other pursuits, yet they resist spending money to join a dating service or on other singles events. An attitude in our society suggests that doing something alone is not as valuable as doing something with someone you love. In order to be a healthy single man, you need to be doing the same things now that you will be doing when you are in a relationship. You can invest in taking out a classified ad or going into counseling to explore your dating patterns. No investment is lost and your efforts will pay off if you make a direct and organized approach to dating. A business would not succeed without advertising or marketing. You need to invest financially in dating if your project is going to succeed. You are investing in yourself and you need to get out there for others to see. Few other ways exist for others to discover you. The advantage of joining a dating service or placing a classified ad is that you are directing your money to the exact group of men you are trying to find. Spending money at bars or parties is not a good business approach and is also not a productive dating approach.

The third goal in finding a mate is investing energy in your dating project. It is too easy to come home from work and collapse on your sofa. You will need to be focused if you want to achieve your goal. This same principle is true for other projects such as starting an exercise program or planting a garden. You will need to set appointments to meet others and stick to your schedule even when you are tired or discouraged. Being realistic about how much energy you have to spend on this project will allow you to set aside available time. When

I was single and dating I was going to graduate school and starting my private counseling practice. I worked three evenings a week and was very busy, but I set aside two evenings a week to return phone calls from my classified ad and two evenings a week to meet men. I let the men I met know I was dating several men and was not looking for a commitment until I found the right person. Many of the men I met were doing the same thing. This approach allowed me to meet almost a hundred men in a year. This experience increased my field of available dating partners.

A good first meeting is to arrange to have dinner. I preferred this for two reasons. First, I often did not have time to eat dinner with my busy schedule and this approach allowed me to meet my nutritional needs. Second, meeting for dinner allowed me to relax and really get to know the person I was meeting rather than rushing through a quick meeting over a drink. Meeting for dinner usually involved two to three hours of conversation in which I learned a great deal about the other person.

I also kept a Dating Journal (see Appendix) with facts and impressions on all of the men I was dating, mainly to organize myself and to prevent memory lapses. I took notes when I was talking with men on the telephone and after meeting them. I rated them in terms of the qualities I was looking for and crossed them off my list if they were not compatible. This approach was not easy, as there were several men who showed interest in me but who were not compatible dating partners. Some of these men were very physically attractive, and this dating approach allowed me to focus on qualities other than physical attributes in choosing a dating partner. I also improved my conversational skills and my ability to remember details. Men responded very positively when I remembered facts about them. I also developed better social skills that allowed me to be more attractive to the men I was meeting. This experience also allowed me to "come out" of my shyness, another closet I decided to leave.

Meeting men and getting to know them before having sex is a very different approach for most gay and bisexual men. My observation is that many gay men pursue sex first in a dating situation because they are insecure about their social skills. It is easy to have sex and falsely believe you are developing closeness and intimacy. As discussed in Chapter 5, I call this type of closeness "pseudo-intimacy." Gay men have not had the opportunity to interact in a nonsexual manner as het-

erosexuals have and this type of interaction feels awkward and un-
usual to them. Also, gay and bisexual men have had to keep their sexual feelings secretive and "flirting" in the general society is strongly
prohibited. This lack of ease interacting with other men often carries
over into interactions with other gay and bisexual men.

Sex can become an easy way of skipping over awkward interactions and fear of rejection. These uncomfortable feelings are very
common in earlier interactions with other men. Holding off on sex
and making conversation is much more relaxing once you become
more socially skilled. Setting up a meeting rather than considering
the first encounter as a date allows you to be more relaxed. You may
discover that you can interact with another man without thinking primarily about sex. You may find many other dimensions in your dating
partners. Developing a safe atmosphere during the first meeting also
allows you and your dating partner a chance to relax without the pressure to have sex. You can then get to know the other person and decide whether you two are a match before you enter into a sexual relationship.

Holding off on sex also allows you to avoid the awkward "morning
after" encounters, when you realize you have slept with a total
stranger or with someone you really do not like. You are not going to
burst if you miss out on a few sexual opportunities. You will survive
and your decision to hold off sexually will pay off. Once you have entered into a sexual relationship, there is the risk that either of you may
become emotionally involved. Sex naturally feels good and you
may convince yourself you feel close when the experience was
purely sexual. Your dating partner may develop a "quick" closeness
with you and you may have difficulty ending the relationship. The relationship remains at a superficial level when you hold off on sex, and
fewer feelings are hurt if you call off dating. If you go slow and remain honest and sincere, your dating partner may remain a friend and
become a part of your social network. Then, you both can assist each
other as you continue your search for the right person. You will also
avoid awkward moments if you see the person later in a social setting.

PART II:
ACTION STAGE—PUTTING ACTION
WITH YOUR WISHES

Chapter 8

Make a Compatibility Inventory

> You can create the perfect relationship for yourself by sitting down and listing the things you want in such a relationship. Meditate on them. Imagine already having such a relationship. Imagine the person you want for a partner. If you are willing for it to happen, someone will come into your life just as you imagine, by this universal law of attraction. Thought creates vibrations which inevitably attract that which is in its image.
>
> Sondra Ray

You may have been indoctrinated in the popular belief that love is all that is necessary to make a relationship succeed. You may have even tried this approach and failed. The truth is that love is not enough. You also need to find a partner who shares your life goals, values, and definitions of a permanent relationship. You need to keep in mind the type of relationship you are creating and the type of person you need to complement yourself. You also need to be the healthy person you believe you are while you are looking for a compatible mate. The other person cannot make you feel happy and complete. You can only find happiness by being healthy and complete within yourself.

Compatibility is perhaps the most important factor in determining the success of a lasting and permanent relationship. It encompasses life goals, values, personal tastes, personal preferences, life expectations, relationship definitions, family goals, future attainments, and perceptions. Some very powerful elements are usually overlooked or neglected during the dating process. I have counseled many couples who did not consider the power of these variables and later realized they were not compatible. They did not discuss their values and goals related to work, career, family, children, finances, vacation preferences, in-laws, and religion. These couples ran into conflict when in-compatibles emerged. Incompatibility is a common relationship prob-lem and is a major contributor to the high divorce rate in the United States. Too many people simply assume that differences will work themselves out if the couple loves each another. They neglect to ex-plore these important aspects of the relationship and discover their importance after it is too late.

You can avoid making similar mistakes by being very clear about what you are looking for right now. If you enter each dating situation with your "compatibility list" in mind, you will be able to rule out those prospects with whom you are not compatible. You can then fo-cus more directly on finding the man you are seeking. Many men who have attended my dating workshops have criticized this rational ap-proach. They perceived it as limiting and unemotional. Nothing could be farther from the truth. For example, if you dream of living in the country with a man who is financially secure, then you will bring this topic up on dates and you will discover he is also moving in this direc-tion. Having your "dream come true" is very emotional and romantic and this approach actually allows you to achieve your dream. If you settle down with an urban man who defines a good time as a trip to a museum or gallery, you will be bored to tears.

You attain your goal today by looking forward. You must start with the end in mind. A well-known fact in farming is the need to focus on a distant point in the field when you are plowing. The lack of focus will lead to a field that looks like a drunken person plowed it. You must look forward when you are dating and not get "caught up in the moment" and give in to momentary gratification. An unfocused ap-proach is fine if you are not looking for a permanent partner. You will need to focus on your goal if you are seeking someone who will join you as a partner for life. If you were looking for a traveling partner to Europe, you certainly would not pick a partner who was seeking to go on an African safari. Rather than finding someone you are attracted to and trying to turn him into the type of man you dreamed of, you need to find the right kind of man and then fall in love. This approach is a very rational one, but you do not have to suspend your feelings. Phys-ical attraction and passion are very important and a happy and lasting relationship will not last if passion is not present. You need both com-patibility and passion to create a lasting and permanent relationship.

This rational dating approach takes a great deal of hard work and organization. You may find it helpful to make a list of the traits you are looking for in a man. The Compatibility Inventory developed in my dating workshops includes most of the factors needed to determine your compatible traits (see chapter's end). Look through this worksheet and check off the traits that you would hope for in an ideal mate. Let yourself fantasize and imagine there are no barriers to finding your truly compatible partner with all the traits you desire. Now that you have made your ideal list, go back through the list and check off those traits that are a "must have." These are the traits that must be present for you to be happy with your selection. These choices are the most important traits you will be looking for and observing in your dating experiences.

Look at your Compatibility Inventory responses. Sit back and examine your ideal list and your must have list. Ask yourself the following questions and be totally honest. Are you seeking someone who is perfect and likely does not exist? Are you realistic in your list of must haves? Are you seeking someone similar to yourself or do you lack many of the same traits? Do you feel you deserve the type of person you have just listed? Now, revise your list based on your discoveries about yourself.

Since you are "in the market," you need to set standards of what you are seeking in a partner and in a relationship. Dating is not simply a prelude to a committed relationship or marriage. Dating is an opportunity to evaluate whether the person you are dating is a good candidate for you. You need to pay attention to your partner's positive and negative characteristics. Ask yourself whether you could live with this person the rest of your life. Remember that you are taking a rational approach to finding a mate and you need to be wary of your emotions. Emotions such as excitement and lust cannot be trusted as reliable markers for a good choice of a partner. Falling in love describes the usual process most people go through when dating. Falling implies losing control and hitting something on the way down and this is the usual experience of most people who fall in love. This is the reason dating gets such bad press. Dating is not the problem, it's the approach that is lacking.

Compatibility with love and not love alone is the key to finding and maintaining a long-term relationship. Knowing the type of person you are looking for is very important if you want to find a long-term relationship. You need to know what you want if you are going to find it. Forget the myth, "There is one special person for everyone." The truth is, there are many men with whom you are compatible. You need to broaden your social outlets and "pool" of available dating partners if you expect to find the right match. Remember that you are not attracted to every man, and you are not being rejected if every man does not ask you out or want to date you. Knowing the characteristics of a compatible person is very important when you are meeting men, but you need to remind yourself you are looking for "relationship material," not simply an attractive man who is attracted to you. You may need to avoid dating someone you are attracted to if you are not compatible with him. This may be hard to do, but you will avoid wasting time on a relationship that will not work.

Pay attention to the "red flags" and warning signs when you are dating. Many people become impatient with the process of healthy dating and settle for someone they are attracted to and who "seems" to meet their criteria. You need to remain aware of potential trouble issues when they arise. For example, I was dating a man who said several times that he was considering a transfer with his company to another state. I chose to overlook this issue in my delusional romantic thinking of, "If we love each other we can work anything out." When I made my list of the traits that I would consider compatible, I decided I wanted a partner who was committed to living in the city I was currently living in. When I was honest with myself, I was able to remind myself that I did not want to relocate at that time and that this person was not a match. This kind of rational decision making is very difficult when your hormones are saying that this is the right man for you. This is the reason you need to keep your list of compatible traits handy when you are dating so that you do not overlook these warning signs.

Not all good things come in attractive packages. You need to be especially aware of potential dangers in a relationship. The most destructive ones are addictions (alcohol, drugs, food, gambling, spending, and sex), severe mental disorders, physical abuse, and deceptiveness. Many individuals become enthralled with someone who appears charming and handsome and they fall prey to an "attractiveness stereotype." This effect was discovered by researchers and refers to the tendency to ascribe positive qualities to someone who is physically attractive (Dion, Berscheid and Walster, 1972). Advertisers, politicians, and the media exploit this attractiveness effect. This research found that people tend to associate more positive qualities with a person who is physically attractive and ascribe more negative qualities to someone who is unattractive. You are vulnerable to this same type of erroneous thinking and you may overlook serious problems in the other person's personality if they are attractive.

Many gay men develop a pattern of rescuing a dating partner and confuse nurturing with love. You may find someone who has "potential" and give into the tendency to "help" the person and thereby gain his love. I call this pattern the "Prince Charming" phenomenon. You believe you can be the one to meet the person's needs and you offer your generous support. This self-deceptive type of thinking pulls for the caregiver in you, as you believe you can help or "rescue" this other person. What you are actually doing is seeking out a dependent partner in order to meet your need to be needed. You may have seen this type of relationship modeled in your family or in the movies. This pattern is a very common scenario for heterosexual couples. Cinderella or Pretty Woman romances are great for popular movies, but they rarely occur in reality.

Rescuers usually find inadequate individuals who need rescuing. The outcome of such rescuing relationships is usually a disaster. The one being rescued is taking advantage of the other person. Even if this is not the case, the dependent one will resent being unequal in the relationship and will resist this role when he is independent. Nobody likes to be reminded that they are weak and helpless and need another person's support to survive. A mutual and interdependent relationship is the healthiest type.

Stick with your compatibility list even when you find the "right guy" and you are ready to get more deeply involved. You need time to test your relationship and discover more about your dating partner. People are very adept at presenting good first impressions, but these impressions do not represent their true personality. Over time, the tendency to hide negative traits will wear off and the person will reveal his true nature. You can then evaluate the quality of the person and the relationship based on your compatible traits. You need to be patient and not give into the tendency to fall in love and thereby lose your objectivity. Do not make a commitment until you are sure or you may have a very difficult time extricating yourself from a bad situation. You may lose several dating partners if you do not quickly commit but you want to lose these partners anyway. A healthy dating partner will accept your feelings and your need to go slow. Someone who rushes you may be only looking for a relationship and may not be open to your needs and desires. This type of person would not make a suitable partner for a long-term relationship.

A compatible mate is not always the best-looking person or the sexiest lover. You have probably experienced that type of person and the relationship probably did not last long. A person of integrity and values will most likely be a person who can commit and accept you even when things are tough. You will not discover if the person you are dating has "staying power" if you rush into a committed relationship. Conflict in the relationship can be a good "testing ground" for both you and your partner's ability to continue in the relationship despite problems. The traits of loyalty, maturity, and an ability to resolve conflicts are the ones that will allow you both to last as a couple.

When I was dating, a man I had just met shared that when he was successful in his company and was making good money and lived in a beautiful house, he and his lover were very happy. But when one of his major contractors claimed bankruptcy and he suddenly lost everything, his lover became distant and left him. He shared with me how disillusioned he was about entering another relationship. The problem was not the relationship, but the person he chose to trust. You need to only trust people who are trustworthy.

Rely on your rational thinking as you are dating and seeking to find a healthy partner. The rational approach is not as exciting as the "head over heels" emotional approach to dating. You will not have butterflies in your stomach, but your vision will remain clear. The saying "love is blind" is very accurate. You lose your objectivity when you fall in love and you need to have a plan going into the dating arena. If you are clear about what you are looking for you will not be as easily swayed when your heart is telling you what to do. This rational approach sounds very boring and may lack romance but it is an approach that works. Passion need not be absent, just not the central aspect of your dating relationships.

Hold off on sex indefinitely if you do not trust yourself. Most people cannot separate sex and their emotions and may confuse a great sexual experience with finding the right person. Nothing could be farther from the truth. There were men with whom I had great sex and whom I thought had all the right qualities, but it was not until I had stopped dating them that I was able to accurately see that they were not a good match. The emotions associated with sex are very strong and tend to cloud judgment. Gay men are especially vulnerable to this kind of error, as many of us have had to hide our sexuality all of our lives. The experience of being accepted and affirmed in a sexual encounter is a very powerful experience. The power of this experience can easily be confused with love. This type of experience is especially common in men who are new to being sexual with men and are coming out. I remember several of these types of experiences when I was coming out and accepting my homosexuality, and I can see now that they were simply adolescent sexual experiences and my choices at that time would not have been healthy ones.

Keep your compatibility list fresh in your mind every time you go out with someone. You may even want to carry it with you or memorize your list. You can then ask questions and bring up topics that will allow your dating partners to reveal their own traits. You need to be discrete as this approach does not work if you view the dating situation as if it were a job interview. You need to be natural about how you bring up each topic so as not to offend your dating partner. Talking about yourself and your own goals is one way to deflect attention away from yourself and onto your dating partner and still gain the information you are seeking. Remember, if you are dating healthy individuals they will be doing the same thing. An information-gathering approach will enable you and him to even further ascertain if you should continue dating. Updating your Dating Journal after each date and rating compatibility will allow you to determine if you should continue dating. You may want to check your list for each individual you meet to give you a guideline of your compatibility. Keep the list for yourself as a guide.

Compatibility Inventory

Place a check next to those traits important to you in choosing a potential partner:

Ideal	Must Have		Ideal	Must Have	
_____	_____	physical attraction	_____	_____	chemistry
_____	_____	similar sexual preferences	_____	_____	spiritual interests
_____	_____	blue-collar job	_____	_____	close in age
_____	_____	older in age	_____	_____	younger in age

_____ _____ values and goals   _____ _____ wants a monogamous relationship

_____ _____ wants to live in the country   _____ _____ wants to live in an urban/suburban area

_____ _____ artistic/creative   _____ _____ similar racial background

_____ _____ similar ethnic background   _____ _____ wants to have or has children

_____ _____ wants a holy union or marriage   _____ _____ same demographic choices (place to live)

_____ _____ resolved sexual identity and orientation   _____ _____ exclusive homosexual preference

_____ _____ bisexual preference   _____ _____ smoker

_____ _____ nonsmoker   _____ _____ alcohol/substance user

_____ _____ nondrinker/non-substance user   _____ _____ spontaneous

_____ _____ planned and organized   _____ _____ regular churchgoer

_____ _____ likes to hang out at bars or clubs   _____ _____ does not like to hang out at bars or clubs

_____ _____ professional/degreed   _____ _____ travels with job

_____ _____ masculine   _____ _____ feminine

_____ _____ androgynous   _____ _____ financially secure

_____ _____ articulate/talkative   _____ _____ HIV+

_____ _____ HIV–   _____ _____ employed full time

_____ _____ athletic   _____ _____ interested in open relationship

_____ _____ sense of humor   _____ _____ _____

_____ _____ _____   _____ _____ _____

_____ _____ _____   _____ _____ _____

_____ _____ _____   _____ _____ _____

Chapter 9

Decide Whom You Want to Be

We must be true inside, true to ourselves, before we can know a truth that is outside us.

Thomas Merton

As stated previously, you are who you attract. This is the most powerful principle of this entire book. You may find you are always attracting men who are emotionally distant. Look at yourself honestly and see if you are also someone who is guarded emotionally. I remember when I was in counseling and I was addressing the problems I had experienced as a single gay man. I had a tendency to attract the wrong kind of man, usually one who was unable to commit and who was emotionally distant. I remember complaining to my therapist about my dating partners and sharing how much I wanted to be in a relationship. She stated, "You don't want to be in a relationship. If you did, you would already be in one." This confrontation led to an insight that totally changed the manner in which I perceived other gay men and myself. I realized that I was actually fearful of commitment and did not trust other men. This was the reason I was attracting my mirror image. I was actually in a "distancing dance" with several partners before I realized that I was attracting exactly what I wanted. When I was honest with myself, I realized that I was fearful of a relationship and the intimacy that goes along with it.

I discovered that loving myself was the key to becoming the right kind of person to attract a healthy partner. The process of changing myself to be the kind of person who was open to intimacy and closeness was difficult. This transformation took several years. I am still involved in this process and the growth did not stop when I found a healthy relationship. This change required me to let go of barriers I had erected to keep others away. I learned to be more giving and less selfish, to experience fear and take risks, and to trust that I can be loved unconditionally. After letting go of many "illusions" about what I thought a relationship was supposed to be, I am now able to accept my partner and our relationship with fewer expectations and fewer conditions. I have let go of the hope that a relationship will make me happy, and instead know that I can create happiness within myself. Being in a relationship is not better than being single, only different. A relationship has challenges and problems that a single life does not have. A relationship is a goal worth pursuing only if one is willing to make sacrifices and experience the growth required to also be a mature and loving partner. This has been the most difficult task I have ever attempted.

The task of developing yourself is an important goal in preparing for a relationship. This goal can include developing an exercise program, taking up new and interesting hobbies or interests, getting involved in volunteer or worthwhile projects, or joining a spiritual fellowship. You may decide to enter counseling to further explore your own problems with relationships. You could take an exotic vacation to broaden your horizons or enroll in adult education classes or learn a new language. Anything you can do to make yourself more interesting and attractive will help your dating and social life. Ultimately, it will give you many more things to talk about on your dates!

A man I was meeting for the first time brought pictures with him of a recent vacation to Hawaii. I had just visited Hawaii and this interaction led to a very long and satisfying conversation. I found I had much in common with this person and we dated several more times. Even though the relationship did not become permanent, the dating relationship we developed was satisfying and I enjoyed getting to know him. Having inviting topics to talk about makes you an interesting person. Many gay and bisexual men are limited in their repertoire of topics. I can't tell you how many men I crossed off my list who only talked about bars, dressing in drag, or the latest gay film. How boring!

Monogamy is one relationship value you may explore. Many people have asked me why I chose to be in a monogamous relationship. I often think of having sex with others and wonder what that would be like. Sometimes I think I am missing out on something by only having one sexual partner and not exploring the variety of sexual experiences an open relationship would allow. It sounds like an exotic existence as in some foreign land where they have different customs and speak a different language—place I'd like to visit but not live.

I think monogamy is my choice because it is less complicated and more comfortable and is simple and easy to understand. My choice is not a highly moral choice even though my morals and values contribute to my decision to remain faithful to my partner. Perhaps I lack the constitution to be involved in an open relationship with all of its inherent complications and rules. It would be too stimulating for me, like riding a roller coaster or river rafting. Exciting in the moment, but a relief when it is over!

My decision to be monogamous is not based on a biological predisposition. I always get upset when people use a biological model to explain their need for multiple partners, as if we are only one step away from the apes and simply obey biological urges. This model is especially offensive to hear when it is used to explain promiscuity in gay men. The biological view that men need to "spread their seed" to many female sexual partners to ensure the survival of their genetic offspring is a heterosexual model. Such an explanation makes the assumption that gay men are heterosexual men "gone wrong" and that we are spreading our seed in places where it could not possibly survive. Gay men cannot reproduce. I think many people use this argument as a justification of their own promiscuous sexual behavior so they do not have to feel guilty. I am not opposed to a person having multiple sexual partners, just offended by the notion that this sexual behavior is viewed as the norm for all gay men. My personal view is that monogamy and promiscuity are preferences and not biological traits.

I think that not choosing monogamy would be a loss for me as well. The notion of being faithful to one partner for life is seemingly so impossible and challenging that the thought of succeeding at this task is in itself exciting. Monogamy is the last great uncharted sexual frontier, as the other variations of human sexuality have been so thoroughly explored. This is especially true for gay and bisexual men.

My partner has also pledged to pursue this great task with me. I owe him my best effort to offer him the same loyalty and faithfulness he offers me. Not having monogamy would be a loss of the fulfillment of ending a life totally committed and tied to another person in a special bond and union. I am not sure I want to give up this experience for having other sexual partners. I content myself with having other sexual partners in my mind and fantasies only and this seems to satisfy my need for sexual excitement and stimulation.

Chapter 10

Develop Your Values and Standards

No matter what age you are, or what your circumstances might be, you are special, and you still have something to offer. Your life, because of who you are, has meaning.

Barbara De Angelis

Many gay and bisexual men describe values such as monogamy and honesty as "heterosexual values," as if there were a different set of values based on sexual orientation. I don't believe that there are different values based on sexuality, gender, or race. Values are values and they are universal even though individuals are unique. Universal values are a constant in our society and form the foundations of our basic institutions. Governments, religious organizations, businesses, and civic organizations all subscribe to a code of values and ethics. Values are a vital part of civilized society and a civilized and ordered life.

Values are often limited to an understanding of morals. The definition of the word value is far broader than simply morals. Synonyms include worth, importance, excellence, desirability, usefulness, esteem, appreciation, and beauty. Values make you who you are. Examples include:

1. honesty,
2. loyalty,
3. supporting those who are weak,
4. valuing life,
5. valuing one's family,
6. loyalty to one's partner,
7. empathy for others' well-being,
8. maintaining safety and security in the environment,

9. independence
10. freedom of speech,
11. maintaining one's health,
12. gaining knowledge, and
13. kindness to others.

There may be other values I have not mentioned, but they are likely variations of these basic values. Values operate as rudders to guide our decisions and our behavior, and are a standard against which we decide how we conduct ourselves in our businesses, friendships, professional associations, neighborhoods, and relationships. Every action is based on a value whether you are aware or not aware of your value.

Other values that are not necessarily negative or bad can often lead to destructive behavior. They can be destructive when they predominate and become an end in themselves. These types of potentially negative values include:

1. hedonism,
2. overemphasis on physical beauty and attractiveness,
3. wealth,
4. power,
5. professional success,
6. societal fame and notoriety,
7. sexual freedom,
8. nonconformity,
9. lack of responsibilities,
10. self-reliance and self-indulgence,
11. excitement,
12. risk taking, and
13. uniqueness.

These values are not necessarily a problem, but they are often the underlying motivation of problems. For example, I may value nonconformity and may herald the Boston Tea Party as an example of the value of nonconformity. However, I create a problem when I refuse to file a tax return because I do not believe citizens should be taxed. The proper use of this value is to combine it with the other values listed and work toward political reform.

The development of a positive self-concept and self-esteem is the end result of practicing one's highest values. You are what you value and self-esteem is the result of behaviors and not feelings. Self-esteem is the value a person places on himself. You are the company you keep. You are what you spend your resources and energy on. You may have heard these words before. This wisdom is as true today as in the past. Many of my clients ask what they can do to develop positive self-esteem. My reply is to identify your values, set positive goals based on your values, and work toward them. The belief that you can become a better person if you work on value-based goals is the starting point. You can achieve your goals when you consciously live out your values. Self-esteem is not a mystery, but it is hard work.

We value things that are important or held in high esteem. If something is of "value," it is rare and costly. Individuals often talk about environments being "value-free" and believe that this is a good thing. People are so ready to call someone "judgmental" these days that many people are trying too hard to not offend anyone. The end result is that many people avoid expressing their values. I do not believe there is such a thing as being value-free. You can value tolerance and a free discussion of issues but this is still a value. We call this value freedom of speech. Everyone has values and the belief that there are no values is erroneous. We also demonstrate our values in what we treat with care. We may only value ourselves and we develop a self-focus. Loving and affirming oneself is a good value; but valuing yourself alone is not a good value. If you value a healthy relationship, you will spend time and energy in this direction, will be willing to spend time in your pursuits, and will also value the individual you date. The manner in which you treat others while dating is the same manner in which you will operate in a long-term relationship.

We usually want to keep something we value. Values are not simply things we claim to have. We work to have values, even when it would be easier or more convenient not to have them. For instance, you may want to have an affair once you are partnered and the other person may appear very attractive. If you value monogamy, you choose not to engage in a sexual relationship outside of your relationship. You actually value dishonesty when you cheat on your partner but profess to value monogamy. Values are not easy to maintain and are like savings accounts. You choose to sacrifice and not engage in immediate gratification when you save money because you are investing in a future return. You lose your values when you abandon them and it takes many years to rebuild your own integrity. If you value yourself, you will not give away your values so easily.

Your friends reflect your values and standards. You would usually choose a company to work with and co-workers who value you and who have similar values. How are relationships any different? Many gay and bisexual men tend to have little discrimination about their friendships. You may feel that you shouldn't judge others, as you are sensitive to the harsh judgment you and others have received in our society. You may tell yourself that you can have fun with one set of friends and develop friendships with others. You may actually believe you can influence those friends who do not share your values. I have found that the opposite is usually true.

If you want to live your values you need to socialize with others who share your values. This does not mean you should reject or be harsh with others who do not share your values. Simply do not develop close relationships with them. You are doing this for yourself, as you do not want to be tempted to violate your values. You need to remember the goal of associating with others with similar values when you are dating. This decision will be especially crucial when you decide on a committed partner. The behaviors and values you are developing while you are dating will be the same ones you adhere to when you are in a relationship.

Self-esteem is intimately related to the values we practice. We feel good about ourselves when we practice behaviors that we view as right and good and we feel bad about ourselves when we practice behaviors that we view as bad and hurtful to others. Values are a basic part of our personality functioning and are not necessarily related to religion or an institution. We develop a positive self-image when our behavior is consistent with the values we espouse. When a discrepancy occurs in these values and our own behavior, a dissonance or discord develops within us. We may attempt to rationalize or justify our behavior, but the harm is done and we lose self-respect and self-worth.

I have worked with many men who have had affairs or cheated on their partners. They hurt their partners and the other person with whom they are cheating. However, they hurt themselves most of all because they lose self-respect. Engaging in an affair and cheating on a partner requires dishonest behavior. You begin to tell one lie, which leads to another and another until you eventually do not even know the truth yourself. Many individuals involved in an affair get caught, as they cannot keep up with their own lies. You also lose respect for yourself as you compromise your values. You may have lied to your cheating partner and promised that you would leave your current partner. You also lose trust, honesty, and monogamy in relationships and become disillusioned.

Relationship Values Inventory

I am a person who wants _____ *in my relationships.* (Check all that apply.)

___ freedom	___ loyalty
___ commitment	___ individuality
___ separate friends	___ shared interests
___ sexual variety	___ multiple sexual partners
___ understanding	___ emotional sharing
___ separate finances	___ shared finances
___ involvement with extended family	___ shared parenting/children
___ competitiveness	___ compatibility
___ similar life goals	___ separate domiciles
___ respect	___ directness
___ open discussion of conflict	___ dominance
___ submission	___ security
___ nonexclusivity	___ tolerance
___ shared social activities	___ shared domicile
___ being "out" as a couple	___ being discrete as a couple
___ adventure	___ spontaneity
___ frequent travel	___ spirituality
___ intellectual compatibility	___ reciprocity
___ mutuality	___ conflict resolution

Chapter 11

Invest in Your Dating Plan

Resolve that whatever you do, you will fling the whole weight of your being into it.

Orison Swett Marden

Many great projects have failed for lack of planning and investment. You have a goal and it is human nature to be impatient to attain the goal or be tempted to cut corners and settle for the first success you experience rather than take a longer course and plan out the goal. Your Dating Journal will be very useful at this time. Think back to your previous dating experiences. What were the behaviors that you liked and disliked? What worked for you in prior dating and what did not? What social skills do you want to develop further and what social skill areas need more improvement? What do you want to convey about yourself when you are on a date? At this point in your dating project, it would be helpful to enlist the help of your friends. They see you interacting in social settings and can give you feedback about the areas you can emphasize and improve on.

Instant success with dating does not exist. You will have many false starts and you need to prepare yourself. The development of healthy social skills is a learning experience and you will have many setbacks. You need to prepare yourself for ups and downs and keep a positive outlook in every encounter. I remember one date in which I was very nervous and I really liked the guy. I tend to become overly talkative or reserved when I really like someone and this time I became very reserved. He asked me questions all night and I did not ask him very much about himself. At the end of the date I could tell we had not really connected and I felt disappointed. I realized that my reservations and shyness had prevented a connection from developing. So much revolves around the initial chemistry and connection, and I realized that I needed to ask more questions and overcome my nervousness when I was on a first date. I used this experience to improve my dating skills.

You are not going to be "discovered" on a date. You must place yourself in locations and situations in which you can meet a long-term partner. This means investing your time and money in romance ads, dating groups, dating services, clubs, and paying for dinner on dates. You need to budget your dating project and plan to spend a good portion of your income (10 to 20 percent) if you really want to find a partner. This may seem like a lot of money, but most of my spending was on paying for my dinner and most of the time my date paid for his own meal. I also attended fund-raisers and political dinners that required a small donation. Church was essentially free other than the offering I gave. The biggest investment was my time and energy.

My Goals for Dating

Examples:

1. I will try to listen more and talk less.
2. I will ask my dating partner questions about his life and look interested.
3. I will avoid controversial issues such as politics and religion.
4. I will not share too much, but will be open and genuine.
5. I will be myself and will not try to impress others.
6. I will not "drop names" and will downplay my accomplishments.
7. I will avoid excessive flirting or innuendoes.
8. I will not have sex on the first date.
9. I will bring up issues shared in our telephone conversations.

Now list your goals and plans:

_____

_____

_____

_____

_____

_____

Hard work and investment of your time and money will pay off in many areas besides dating. I had minimal social skills prior to dating and I was very reserved in social settings. Usually I would sit back and wait to jump in the conversation and someone else would beat me to the punch line. I was also very shy when talking to people I did not already know and would usually avoid this type of situation at all costs. Answering and placing a classified romance ad allowed me to develop better social skills and better social interactions in many areas, and I found that I was much more comfortable and outgoing. I began to make more contacts professionally which were very rewarding financially and personally. After finding a business partner, I moved my practice and formed new professional relationships. I also performed professional marketing for a private psychiatric hospital and this job considerably improved my social skills. The dating experience had boosted my self-confidence in many other social situations. Even if I had not found a long-term partner, I would have been very pleased with the outcome of my new social skills.

Another approach, which allowed me to stay focused during my dating project, was reading books on dating skills. Several of these are listed in the bibliography of this book. Knowledge truly is power, and the more information you have, the better equipped you will be to face your task. The many years of college and graduate training seemed excessive at the time I was enduring them, but I see now the reason for such extensive training. I would not feel confident to perform my job as a therapist had I not been equipped academically and personally. The months of healthy dating you will experience will be well worth the time and effort when you end up in a lasting relationship. Remember your ultimate goal when you are tempted to give into self-pity or discouragement.

Chapter 12

Dealing with Failure and Setbacks

Pain in itself is not an evil to be avoided at all costs. Pain is rather a teacher from whom we can learn much.

John Powell

Dating is a learning process and you will learn through trial and error. You have never been trained to date in a healthy manner and you have probably never had any exposure to healthy dating between two men. Even if you had been trained to date in a healthy manner, most dating lessons are learnd in actual situations. This book is only a guide and cannot replace the actual experience of dating. You need to plan to have many learning experiences and you need to view these experiences as a natural part of dating. Experiential learning occurs in any new behavior you develop. You would not expect to sit down at a piano and play it perfectly with no lessons and no practice. Nor should you expect to have perfect dating skills from the beginning. Unfortunately, few people recognize the need to develop and practice dating and relationship skills. Give yourself time to experience the learning curve with healthy dating.

Personalizing your setbacks and failures will hinder the development of new dating skills. Personalizing is the mental process of blaming yourself or some personal quality for the success or failure of a particular situation. It occurs when you assume that the outcome of each dating experience can be attributed to your traits or qualities. Many people do not like dating because they tend to personalize. They believe dating will reveal their weaknesses and flaws and they will be rejected. Deep down they believe they are unworthy and inadequate. This belief can often be erroneous and one founded on minimal evidence. I have counseled many handsome and intelligent men who thoroughly believed they were inadequate. I have also worked with many men who were not as physically attractive but who realized they could achieve a satisfying relationship. Many gay and bisexual men have bought into the belief that sex and relationships are easy and come only to good-looking young men. Personalizing is based on the belief that you must fit the "young and beautiful" gay stereotype to find a partner. When a dating situation does not work out, you may utilize this type of distorted thinking and defeat yourself by personalizing your failures.

Negative thinking can create a self-fulfilling prophecy. If you tell yourself you will never find anyone and will be alone the rest of your life, you will come to believe this prophecy when a dating experience does not go well. This negative thinking not only keeps you depressed and feeling inadequate, but it also keeps you from learning from the negative experience. You need to maintain an objective stance toward yourself if you are going to learn form your setback and improve your skills. Calling someone in your dating support system is helpful if you are prone to negative thinking. These people can offer you objective and supportive feedback and prevent you from falling into the trap of the self-fulfilling prophecy.

Chapter 13

Watch Out for the Hidden Dangers

Your soul is oftentimes a battlefield, upon which your reason and your judgment wage war against your passion and your appetite.

Kahlil Gibran

As with any single person, you will need to be aware of the potential dangers involved in dating. Many single people experience these dangers and only learn after a bad experience that they could have prevented the harm. You do not need to learn from experience to avoid these dangers and you can learn from others' experience. The most common dangers include sexual compulsivity, unsafe sex and infection, gay and bisexual married men, committed gay and bisexual men in "unhappy" relationships, closeted men, "Daddy" types, "Gold-digger" types, sadomasochism, dependent types, and alcohol and drug abuse.

Sexual Compulsivity

Sexual addiction or sexual compulsivity is an epidemic among gay and bisexual men. This epidemic is a reality many therapists see every day, but one which most people do not want to face. Much of the stereotypes of gay and bisexual men have been derived from the promiscuous behavior of sexual addicts so this is a politically incorrect subject. However, the existence of high rates of sexual addiction is documented by the large number of men seeking sexual-addiction treatment, the high rate of arrests for sexual offenses involving sex in public places, and in the high rate of HIV transmission. I have always wondered why people do not assess for sexual addiction when a person is diagnosed with HIV infection, as this virus can be transmitted through sexual contact.

As a person entering the "dating world" you need to be aware of this danger. Many people will lie about their sexual behavior or will fail to disclose all sexual behaviors because they fear rejection. You will need to directly address the subject but you also need to maintain a healthy skepticism as you date someone and learn more about his sexual behavior and background. Sexual addicts develop a "double life" and learn how to present a positive image to people whom they do not wish to disclose their sexual acting out. Many of my clients actually travel to out-of-town cities and foreign countries to sexually act out and to avoid encountering people in their social network. Sexual addicts will not usually report their behavior honestly to you unless in therapy or in support groups. You will perceive the sexual addiction if you go slow and are objective and do not allow love to make you blind to this potential danger in your dating partner.

The signs of sexual addiction are numerous and easy to detect if you are willing to get to know a dating partner. Look for excessive activity on the Internet, listen to comments made by friends and past dating partners, be wary of inconsistencies and omissions of important sexual information, and ask questions that are very direct. Maintain a healthy skepticism and carefully assess his responses. If he is sexually addicted, you will receive vague answers and may even encounter some irritable responses as a result of your directness. You may also hear rationalizations, such as "Straight people think we have to have the same morals as they do and I think we are free from their morals and values." Other rationalizing statements include, "Gay men are usually more sexual than women and we need variety" or "People too quickly judge a person by their sexual behavior or sexual history." Such comments will reveal the person's thinking that supports sexually addictive attitudes and behaviors.

Sexual addiction has disastrous consequences and you need to take this issue very seriously. Sexual addicts are not bad people. They have a disease that is similar to alcoholism and they are unable to control their sexual behavior. They are also in denial about the addictive nature of their behavior and will not be aware of their addiction and risk-taking behavior unless they have entered support groups or therapy. Treatment is available and many therapists specialize in treating sexual addiction and compulsivity. You can easily find a therapist by calling psychiatric and chemical dependency treatment centers in your area. Sexual addicts can be successfully treated on an outpatient basis and for low cost. Many therapy groups composed of gay and bisexual men exist that address the client's sexual-orientation issues as well as the sexual addiction. Sex Addicts Anonymous (SAA) and Sex and Love Addicts Anonymous (SLAA) are free and offer additional support in developing a recovery lifestyle. Many of the support groups also have gay and bisexual groups so more open discussions can occur.

Unsafe Sex and Infection

The reality of HIV infection and AIDS has been with the gay community for almost twenty years. Many people have become sensitized to this issue and it is treated casually. You may have heard your friends say, "Almost everyone is HIV positive, so I am going to assume that any man I date is positive," or "Since so many men are HIV positive, I guess I cannot expect to find a man who is HIV negative." Pressure within the gay community can cause you to accept a dating partner who is HIV positive, as rejecting him is perceived as prejudice and homophobia. Your beliefs about HIV infection are very important to your choice of sexual behaviors. Your dating and sexual choices are your individual preference as you date and seek a partner. You need to be honest with yourself if you do not want to date someone due to his HIV status. If you assume it is no big deal, then you will get in over your head and possibly become emotionally involved with someone before you realize you cannot handle his illness. If you are honest about your feelings from the start, you will prevent hurting others and wasting your time with dating partners who are not compatible.

Being aware of your attitudes regarding HIV status is important regardless of your own HIV status. Some HIV-positive men do not want to date other HIV-positive men. The choice to be in a relationship with a man who is HIV positive requires some careful consideration of your values and willingness to give selflessly. You need to value safe sex and be comfortable with it. Unprotected oral or anal sex with an infected partner represents a very high risk. You need to ask yourself if you are willing to take this kind of risk. Most HIV-positive partners will not want to engage in these behaviors even if you are willing to take the risks involved.

Can you assume a caretaker role if your partner becomes ill for an extended period of time? Most insurance plans do not cover home health care and this can be very expensive. Your partner may also be on disability and may not work. Can you assume financial responsibility in the relationship if your partner needs your assistance? Do not fool yourself that "love conquers all." In my years of counseling HIV-positive men, I have had numerous cases in which the HIV-negative partner left my client who was HIV positive when the HIV-positive partner became sick or disabled. This type of rejection is especially hurtful and hypocritical. Be honest with yourself and avoid this type of hurt.

Disclosure of your HIV status, positive or negative, is important early in the dating relationship. A general rule about disclosure is to tell your dating partner your HIV status prior to having sex or if he asks you about it directly. Having sex without revealing your HIV status is a form of abuse even if you are practicing safe sex. You need to treat your dating partner with care and concern if you expect to find a healthy partner. Your partner may also become angry if you do not tell him until after having sex that you are HIV positive. This type of behavior may be perceived as deceptive. An HIV-positive man who does not disclose his HIV status is usually afraid of rejection and likely has low self-esteem. This negative self-concept may also turn off your dating partner. Telling your status openly reveals honesty and a willingness to face others' negative reactions. "Coming out" as an HIV-positive man is a freedom similar to coming out as a gay or bisexual man. Do not deprive yourself of the opportunity to be free from your fears of rejection and abandonment. Being honest will also give you information about your dating partner; a healthy individual will have very strong feelings about this issue and will be open to processing them with you.

Gay and Bisexual Married Men

Surveys show that as many as 15 percent of all men have had sex with both men and women, and most are in relationships with or are married to women. Bisexuals do not socialize at gay bars or groups. They usually seek out sexual partners in discrete locations such as gyms, rest rooms, and parks. Some bisexual men have decided to not have sex with their wives, but instead to develop a sexual relationship outside the marriage. Many of these men do not plan to divorce and may be attempting to "have their cake and eat it too." I have counseled many men and couples in these situations and their predicament is agonizing. Children are often involved and complicated custody issues arise. Many of the bisexual men are actually gay and are not ready to come out as gay men. Some bisexual men are truly bisexual and simply do not want to give up the security and esteem they have as husbands and fathers. Whatever the situation, these men are not ready to develop any type of relationship with you. They need to resolve their sexual orientation and marital issues prior to engaging in a relationship with another person. Many of them will not have the judgment or maturity to do so and you must set limits with such a dating partner. You can be a very helpful friend and allow the person to talk about his feelings but be careful about giving into the temptation to have sex with him. These bisexual men have been deprived of closeness and sexual intimacy with other men for most of their adult lives and they may be very eager to have sex. They may be very good-looking and nurturing, but do not give in to their seduction.

You may find you are more attracted to "straight-appearing" men. This type of attraction pattern may represent unresolved homophobia or unresolved issues of separation and approval with a father figure. I have worked with many clients to understand why they are so attracted to married bisexual men when they repeatedly find themselves used sexually and then abandoned. The best option for you with such an individual is to be a good friend and not exploit him in his confusion. Offer him referrals for support groups and counseling. He may eventually be able to resolve his situation and become a healthy dating partner. Many free support groups are available for married gay and bisexual men that can assist them in resolving such situations.

Committed Gay and Bisexual Men in "Unhappy" Relationships

Many men are dissatisfied in their current relationship and are looking for someone else. For various reasons, they are still entangled with their prior partner and they may actually represent their ex-partner as a "roommate" with whom they have no romantic involvement. Such individuals have many problems and may be love-addicted or dependent personalities. They are unable to be alone and will look for someone to "rescue" them from an unhappy relationship rather than venture out on their own and face their aloneness. Such a man may flatter you and attempt to convince you that you are the one for him.

He may make many promises to leave his ex-partner and he may want to "keep you in the wings."

Involvement with a man already in a relationship is often based on a fantasy of having an affair with a partnered man. The possible harm to the other party needs to be considered in your decision to be involved with him. You may assume that your dating partner is being honest with you about his ex-partner's feelings but you really do not know the truth about the situation. You could cause a great deal of harm to the other person if you display your relationship with this dating partner and the ex-partner sees the two of you together. Also, this type of dating partner is not ready to commit again and may be on the rebound. You may find a tendency in yourself to "rescue" this dating partner from his unhappy relationship especially if the ex-partner has been abusive or dysfunctional. This type of response is characteristic of codependency. You may need to be needed in order to feel loved. You will attract a man who is needy and dependent and this type of individual may not be the type of man you are looking for.

Also, a man who cheats on a partner will also cheat on you. I always find it amazing when an individual is having an affair with a person in a relationship and really believes that his partner could actually be faithful and loyal. Values are expressed in our behavior and not in our words. You may be caught up in a romantic fantasy that has nothing to do with reality if you are falling for this type of man. You may also have a need to steal away a partner from someone else as a means of gaining a sense of superiority or desirability. You may need to look at the gains you are seeking in pursuing such a relationship that is so obviously unhealthy. Your need to have an emotionally unavailable partner who is never truly committed may relate to unresolved issues from your past and childhood.

Closeted Men

Most gay and bisexual men have dealt with the difficulty of being closeted and afraid to reveal their homosexuality. You may be tempted to help a dating partner in this process only to find that you are a "stepping-stone" relationship for him. Men who are coming out are similar to adolescents emotionally and they are not ready for a committed relationship. They may say they want a relationship, but many men who are coming out may be simply attempting to find a partner as quickly as they can to avoid the discomfort of meeting other gay men. They may seek a relationship to actually remain closeted and only be "out" to another man.

Again, you can be a good friend to someone recently out, but be careful not to fall into a trap of attempting to ease his pain of coming out. Each of us must take the coming-out process at our own speed. You can be a very good role model and sounding board for ideas but do not allow yourself to get too close. Some men who are coming out have the tendency to be overly sexual due to the many years of sexual deprivation they have experienced. It is possible to exploit this person's vulnerability and take advantage of his naiveté. The end result may be disillusionment for him and you may actually drive him back into the closet. Developing a healthy nonsexual relationship while he is coming out will allow him to gain the support he needs while he is accepting himself and taking risks to reveal his sexual orientation to others. After he has been out for a year or so, he will have worked through many of his issues and will be ready for a relationship that is meaningful and stable.

"Daddy" Types

Many gay and bisexual men find that they are attracted to younger men. Though some men have a legitimate preference for younger men, some men have a belief that they need to have a young and sexy partner to be happy and valuable. They tend to fall into the same traps as heterosexual men who seek younger women. They may use their stability and financial security as "bargaining chips" in the dating game and this approach may actually work for them. Be very careful of this type of offer as there are usually many strings attached. You need to give yourself time to get to know this person and discover if their attraction to you is based on more than youth and attractiveness.

On the other hand, many older and younger men find that they are in love and make a good match. This issue still needs to be addressed early on, as there will be many obstacles in your relationship if you decide to commit to each other. For example, your partner may be the same age as your parents and this may create a problem with them, your friends may not prefer the company of older individuals and this may create conflicts with them, or you may also have a hard time relating to an older person due to style differences between generations. Generational differences are certainly a factor when two individuals have a great difference in their ages. You also need to look ahead and perceive the relationship five, ten, and twenty years down the road. Will you feel comfortable with a partner who is retired long before you are? Are you comfortable with the possibility of caregiving if your partner becomes ill or disabled? Can you deal with his death occurring before your own? These questions need to be asked when a great age difference exists so that you will be prepared should these issues arise.

"Gold-Digger" Types

The other side to men who are seeking young men to take care of is the younger men who are looking for partners to take care of them. These types of men may not reveal this as a goal when dating and you will need to carefully discern if your dating partners are seeking financial gain in dating you. Avoid this type from the beginning by establishing that both parties will pay their own way. This type of dating will be a turn-off to the "gold-digger" type and he will eventually pull away. If this strategy does not work, explore his past relationships and discover if he was with men who were financially secure and who paid his expenses. You can also hear his need for financial security in his statements about future goals and plans.

A younger man may be a big temptation for a man who has always dreamed of having a younger good-looking partner. In our society, gaining such a spouse is a symbol of superiority and virility. Such a selection supports superficial values. This behavior is common in older heterosexual men who divorce their wives and marry young women. This dynamic was played out in the recent movie, *The First Wives Club,* in which the older women faced the rejection of their husbands for younger women. This decision was made by one character despite the fact that he still loved his older wife.

Repeating the same mistakes of heterosexual couples is not very progressive and serves to reinforce the ideal that only youth and beauty are to be prized. This strategy could work against you when your younger lover finds someone else. You may have a lover who will be unfaithful, as he is sexually desirable to others. You will need to evaluate whether you can weather several affairs and live in a pretend world rather than face the reality that you have a lover who loves only your money. You may also be in for a rude awakening should anything ever happen to your money because you will probably lose your lover.

Sadomasochism

First I want to make clear that leather and dominance-submission sexual behaviors are not unhealthy if mutual consent exists and no harm comes to either party. I realize that leathermen clubs and groups sponsor wholesome bondage practices; I am not addressing these individuals. On the other hand, a segment of the gay community is into sadomasochism. This type of sexual behavior associates pain and degradation with sexual arousal. I have counseled several individuals who were dating and found a partner who was into this type of sex. They found it intriguing even though there was pain and risk at times. Their naiveté was surprising and disturbing to me given the information we have today about the dangers of S/M sex.

First, abusive S/M sex is not gay sex, as heterosexuals have been into this type of sex for centuries. It was likely practiced by slaveowners and on conquered peoples in the past. Historical accounts of the caesars of Rome abound with examples of abusive S/M sex. The "costumes" of black leather are also not unique to gay men and have been worn by bikers and "outlaws" for generations. Leather is a personal preference. Some men happen to like leather and are gay, and for them, the two preferences intertwine. My point in this discussion is that you do not need to accept abusive behavior simply because you are gay. If you do not prefer this type of sex or behavior, it is okay to say so. You are not rejecting the gay community in doing so, no matter what others would have you believe.

You also need to be careful as people have been "accidentally" killed during S/M sex that went wrong. In a recent case, a gay man in a midwestern town had S/M sex with a bisexual man and killed him during their sexual ritual. The gay man was charged with murder and many gay groups criticized the case. What was not discussed was that these two men were likely caught up in this abusive form of sex and were unwilling or unable to practice it safely. The degradation of S/M sex reinforces the same rejection many gay and bisexual men have felt all of their lives. Engaging in S/M sex is a form of reenacting abuse trauma for many men who want others to denigrate and humiliate them. They have associated feelings of self-loathing with their sexuality and converted it into a harmful sexual practice. This type of sexuality is certainly not healthy emotionally and has its physical dangers as well.

Dependent Types

Dependency and love addiction is rampant in the gay and lesbian community. You may discover many men who latch on to you from the very first encounter. Part of this reaction is due to the trauma of being closeted sexually for so much of their lives. These individuals form dependencies when they perceive they have found a potential mate. Some men are more severely affected and may actually form an enmeshed attachment and may seek to stalk and harass you if you do not accept them. A client told me about this potential relationship danger. He stated he and his partner were at a local gay bar and another man became fixated on his partner. His partner was not interested in him sexually, and the other man would not take no for an answer. The obsessed man grabbed the partner's pants and pulled them down as the couple attempted to leave the bar. This led to a fight between the two parties and the police were called.

This individual was so obsessed with having sex, he assaulted someone when rejected. No real possibility of rape existed, but the person's dangerousness was clear. Dependent types are not usually so obvious. Initially, they appear very warm and giving, successful and independent. This dependency may not surface until you attempt to back off emotionally or set some boundary he finds intolerable. For example, you may want to call only two to three times a week and he calls you daily, or you may not want to plan every weekend or evening around him and you may find he expects you to spend all of your free time with him.

I was very much the dependent type when I first began to date. I realize now that I had not resolved a personal issue of my father's lack of affection toward me when I was a child, and had not become completely comfortable with being a gay man. I sought desperately for someone to love me, hoping that this love would vanquish my past feelings of rejection and would also ease the discomfort of being gay. Having someone in my life was my constant goal and I had a series of very unsuccessful dating relationships. I realized that I was attracting men similar to my father while pushing away healthy partners with my dependent behavior.

After several negative dating experiences, I sought counseling and realized I was a love addict. This awareness was a turning point in my acceptance of myself and in my dating life. Love addiction was a very difficult concept to grasp, as much of my behavior appeared to be healthy dating. However, I could never get enough attention from men. My desperation left me alone and feeling rejected. I realized that love addiction could be as powerful an obsession as any other addiction. My view of love was very distorted by my own unresolved issues. After I began to delve into my childhood pain, I learned to love the "child within" who had always felt neglected and unloved, to speak loving statements to myself, and to develop a loving relationship with myself. I realized I had never loved myself and therefore was ill-equipped to love another person. Facing my fears of being single and being involved in a gay lifestyle helped me to decide to be honest with myself and let go of the "mask" of being so self-assured. I learned that I had a lot to offer another man and did not have to be desperate. I met my partner several months after completing this therapy. He and I saw the same therapist for premarital counseling as well.

Alcohol and Drug Abuse

A great deal of alcohol and drug abuse exists among gay and bisexual men and estimates vary that between one out of five and one out of three gay and bisexual men regularly abuse alcohol and drugs. A recent phenomenon of the gay community is the advent of "circuit parties." These events are held all around the country and a great deal of illegal drug use occurs. The most popular drugs at the moment appear to be methamphetamine, cocaine, Ecstasy, Special K (an animal tranquilizer), and "poppers" (an inhalant). These substances have been around for years and have now become part of the bar and club scene. Many gay men have become addicted to them. Though none of these substances is physically addictive in terms of creating tissue dependence (as with alcohol and heroin), they are highly psychologically addictive. Many are powerful disinhibitors, and they lower inhibition for a person to engage in risky sexual behavior. Alcohol abuse has long been considered a primary risk factor for HIV infection, as it places you at high risk to engage in unsafe sexual behaviors and thus become infected.

In *Life Outside*, Michelangelo Signorile, a writer for *OUT* magazine, analyzes the development of the dance party phenomenon, which has become associated with promiscuous sex, alcohol, and substance abuse. He states that this culture is affecting men of all types whether they attend parties or not. Also associated with the circuit scene are HIV-positive men who are taking steroids and have developed highly muscular physiques. These men may appear healthy on the outside but this veneer is very deceptive. The ideal of the handsome, muscular, sexually promiscuous, substance-abusing gay or bisexual man is being celebrated at these parties even though this idealization would be denied by many of those attending.

When you are dating be sure to ask questions about your dating partner's involvement in the circuit scene. Assume the worst before you determine that a dating partner is healthy. Many gay and bisexual men are beginning to speak out against this type of lifestyle as being destructive to the participants and to the gay rights movement. Signorile has been harshly criticized as judgmental and moralistic in his analysis of gay and bisexual men in the circuit parties. One sad outcome is that many men may perceive muscular HIV-positive men as desirable and may seek to have sex with them or seek to be like them. This phenomenon is likely responsible for much of the continued HIV infection in the gay community, despite the money spent on safe-sex education by government agencies.

Chemical dependency is an illness similar to sex addiction and there are excellent treatment options available if you or your dating partner realize you need help in getting sober. Programs are available for HIV-positive individuals in which treatment or counseling may be free or very low cost. A person who wants help has no reason not to receive it. The major obstacle is the denial that accompanies chemical dependency as the addict does not perceive that he has a problem requiring treatment. I directed an intensive outpatient recovery program for those with chemical dependency and only 5 to 10 percent willingly sought treatment. The other clients were usually forced into treatment reluctantly by partners, probation officers, judges, or employers.

The myth that you cannot help addicts or alcoholics unless they want help is not true. Given the opportunity to receive treatment, many addicted individuals do realize they have a problem and decide to receive treatment. An "intervention" is a confrontation in which those who love and care for the addict or alcoholic confront him about his illness. Interventions are highly effective and usually result in the addicted person receiving help. Many treatment centers provide low-cost intervention services for those who are willing to reach out to their addicted friends and partners.

Chapter 14

Keep Up Your Momentum

> To be organized and efficient, to live wisely, we must daily delay gratification and keep an eye on the future; yet to live joyously we must also possess the capacity, when it is not destructive, to live in the present and act spontaneously.
>
> M. Scott Peck

Avoid the temptation to let up on your dating goals when no immediate results occur. Healthy dating requires a steady and diligent investment of your time and energy and immediate gratification is not guaranteed. I have had several clients who exclaimed their frustrations and shared how easy it was to find a sexual partner but yet how difficult it was to find a dating partner. You may experience the same kind of disappointment or frustration. Many people try a new behavior and give up when they do not attain immediate results. I think the basic problem with such individuals is their impatience. You will need to be very patient as you are going through the dating process in order for your behavioral changes to work. Many people make a great deal of change and give up right when they are about to have a breakthrough. Keep your momentum going and expect the best out of every dating encounter. Your positive attitude will carry you forward when you are discouraged.

Avoid the temptation to engage in casual sex while you are dating and have not found a lasting relationship. You do not need any distractions to keep you from your final goal. In my Finding a Lover for Life Workshop, one participant shared that he went to the baths for sex when he did not have a date. He did not realize he was using precious time to have casual sex when he could have been out socializing and meeting healthy men. He also did not realize that he would be unlikely to meet a healthy dating partner at the baths, and did not consider how some men might view his behavior if known to them. Most relationship-oriented men do not engage in casual sex, as they are seeking lasting relationships. You also need to be careful not to subscribe to the "men are pigs" mentality and give in to sexual promiscuity when you become frustrated. The time to pursue your goals even harder is during times of frustration. If you allow every setback to literally "set you back" then you will be farther and farther from your goal of finding a partner. Visualize your goal and keep going even when the going gets rough.

The use of sex to cope with loneliness or to offer a boost to your self-esteem is very unhealthy. As you develop healthy dating patterns, you will begin to change the way you view your sexuality. You may have considered sex as a way of having fun or gaining pleasure. Although these are normal and healthy ways to view sex, the overemphasis on the pursuit of sex often leads to promiscuity and sex with little meaning. You may have used sex to cope with feelings of inadequacy you felt as a gay or bisexual man growing up in an oppressive culture. This is a self-defeating use of sex, as the men you encounter will also be seeking to "use" you for their own gratification. You will leave the encounter with little or no lasting satisfaction.

A healthy view of sex is one in which sex is used to connect with another human being at a spiritual or meaningful level. This does not mean that sex must be only between two committed individuals. You can develop a healthy sexual self while you are single. Such positive changes in your sexuality while you are single will allow you to be committed when you find a partner. You will also need to continue to develop your personal and social interests during these periods in order to keep up the momentum. You may hesitate to accept an invitation to a party or a social gathering as you may want to keep your calendar open "just in case." This approach is actually more likely to keep others from contacting you. You are preventing yourself from meeting other available men by allowing yourself to become socially isolated. You need to keep your goal to find a relationship in the foreground and seek to develop your interest during these dry spells. The most destructive behavior you can choose is to give up and stay at home just because you do not have a date planned.

These dry periods can be periods of great individual growth and self-development. As mentioned previously, it is very important for you to develop a healthy relationship with yourself if you hope to attract a healthy partner. Take time to pursue leisure interests or hobbies you enjoy so that you do not return to the mentality that your life is not complete without a romantic partner. Self-pity is your worst enemy and will lead to loneliness and depression. Remember the interests that bring you satisfaction. These activities will enrich you and will keep you from becoming bored and discouraged. You can have a great life as a single person if you remember the positive aspects of being single. Keep up the momentum of being happy and self-fulfilled, as this is a major factor in attracting healthy and compatible partners. The less you feel you need a dating partner, the more attractive you will appear. Momentum is everything, so do not give in to lethargy and complacency.

PART III:
COMPLETION STAGE—
FINDING AND KEEPING
A LASTING RELATIONSHIP

Chapter 15

Gather Information on the Date

The road to the heart is the ear.

Voltaire

You are dating and having fun, but you are wondering if this is the right guy. Now that you are finally meeting healthy potential partners, you need to gain as much information as quickly as you can. The best approach is to start out slow and hold off on sharing too much on a first date. Sharing too much can create discomfort in most individuals, as they may not be ready to self-disclose so openly. As you date several times, begin to bring up various topics indirectly and listen very carefully to your date's responses. For example, if you comment on how you would like to have children one day and your date states that he has never wanted children, you need to take him seriously. Too many men think they can change their partners' minds on important issues after they are committed. People rarely change their minds on such important issues.

Keep up entries in your Dating Journal. Remember that you are working on a project and not just randomly interacting and selecting a dating partner. Your Dating Journal serves many purposes. First, if you are successful in developing a broad social network, you will be meeting many different people. Don't trust your memory; a Dating Journal will allow you to keep records of your telephone conversations and initial reactions. When you meet or see the person again, you will be equipped with personal information. Such details are important to that person and remembering details makes others feel special. Attention to detail will be noticed and will increase your level of attraction to the other person. Second, your Dating Journal allows you to think about and record your impressions of the other person. What did you find attractive? What did you find interesting or unique? What did you find offensive or uninteresting? Did you perceive any red flags or warning signs that you need to note and be aware of? What personal information was attractive to you? What do you want to learn more about? Recording these types of notes in your journal will allow you to be more focused and will also allow you to not forget important information. I keep detailed notes about my clients because I cannot afford to forget personal information about them. Keeping information available will allow you to keep track of your experiences while you are dating and will allow you to better evaluate your decisions.

Remember your Compatibility Inventory and be careful to avoid the temptation to fall for good looks or good sex. As discussed earlier, you will want to keep your goal focused on the type of person you feel will be a good match. Gathering information in a casual manner will allow you to determine if this person has many of the traits you are looking for. Remember that you are not looking for the perfect mate but someone who will have similar goals, values, and lifestyle choices. If you get too excited when you meet someone special, you run the risk of forgetting your compatibility list and giving in to your emotions. You may think that if it feels right it must be right. Keep in mind how this approach has led to many poor choices in the past and rely on your list of compatible traits. Dating several men at a time is also a good way to evaluate which men are compatible. If you use this approach, you can determine before you become too emotionally involved which person is best suited to be your ideal mate.

Chapter 16

Open Up and Let Others In

The genius of communication is the ability to be both totally honest and totally kind at the same time.

John Powell

Selling yourself on a date does not mean you are being fake. The natural tendency is to present an overly positive impression on initial dates. Psychologists call this phenomenon "impression management," and it is the tendency to present your most positive and favorable traits (see Asch, 1946; Goffman, 1959). Such a strategy occurs when you are seeking to gain favors or positions from another person. We usually do not worry about our impression with our family and friends, as they already know us and we are sure of their acceptance. With people we have just met, we are uncertain if they will like us and accept us and we "put on a front."

Self-disclosure is revealing oneself to others. When we self-disclose, we reveal our private experiences—our past experiences, our fears, our desires, our plans, and our fantasies. A lack of self-disclosure has been found to be associated with loneliness and poor emotional adjustment (see Chelune, Sultan, and Williams, 1980; Berg and Peplau, 1982; Davis and Franzoi, 1986). People who fail to self-disclose do not form close and intimate relationships with others and remain superficial and distant in their interactions (see Franzoi and Davis, 1985). Research on self-disclosure has found that individuals reported increased attraction and liking when the other person self-disclosed (see Worthy, Gary, and Kahn, 1969). Increased self-disclosure appears to lead to increased likability and attraction. Self-disclosure was also found to stimulate self-disclosure in the other person (see Jourard, 1959; Worthy, Gary, and Kahn, 1969). This is a fact that therapists have known for a long time as they use self-disclosure to allow clients to increase their own self-disclosure. This interaction is based on the principle of reciprocity.

A basic social norm is to return to someone as he or she has given to you (see Gouldner, 1960). A basic human trait is to have balance and equity in relationships. Therefore, self-disclosure is a great way for you to become attractive and likable on a date and is also a great way to learn more about the other person.

Although self-disclosure is a natural tendency of all humans, this approach can also backfire in a dating situation. Certainly you do not want to be overly disclosing, as you will appear to have poor boundaries. Also, you do not want to be so distant that you appear aloof and unreachable. Self-disclosure will allow you to reveal your specific goals and values, which will allow the other person to assess if you are an appropriate partner for him, and also causes the other person to self-disclose. You will then gain information about him that will allow you to assess if you are compatible.

Gender differences also may affect the perception of an individual who self-discloses. Men are socialized not to self-disclose, as this is perceived as weakness and vulnerability (see Helgeson, Shaver, and Dyer, 1987). Also, men are accustomed to doing things together in their friendships rather than talking and sharing with one another (see Caldwell and Peplau, 1982; Reis, Senchak, and Solomon, 1985). Self-disclosure from a man may be perceived as feminine or as a trait of someone who is emotionally unstable. Conversely, self-disclosure is also associated with better social adjustment (see Jourard, 1971). Although gay and bisexual men may believe they are emancipated from gender socialization in a heterosexual culture, they are mistaken. The years of socialization by our fathers, teachers, coaches, ministers, and friends has a cumulative effect and the process of resocialization as a gay and bisexual man can take many years.

The task for "liberated" gay and bisexual men is to challenge the false beliefs about men in our culture and begin to develop feminine and masculine traits. This process can be especially difficult for gay and bisexual men who have been closeted and who have worked very hard not to appear gay. For many men, suppression of their femininity becomes a strategy to avoid detection of their sexual orientation by bigoted heterosexuals. You may want to consider joining a support group or therapy group of gay and bisexual men who are addressing these issues as a means of allowing yourself to change your interactions with men.

I conduct several groups composed of gay and bisexual men and resocialization is a major part of the change process. The men find that they have difficulty opening up and sharing their weaknesses, and may actually be very critical of others and themselves when these weaknesses are perceived. They also find great relief when they open up and share their feelings and gain support from others. Many gay and bisexual men have been so isolated and detached from others due to the difficulties in dealing with society's rejection that they are very closed and shut down emotionally. Allowing their emotions to emerge allows for a great deal of healing and change to occur. Gay and bisexual men have few skills in interacting and forming relationships with other men as sexual and dating partners. This dynamic may explain why there is a tendency to have sex too quickly. For many men, having sex with other men is the only way they know how to relate. Many gay and bisexual men who think they are liberated sexually are very inhibited emotionally.

Self-disclosure is a "two-edged sword" that can both enhance your interactions with others and can also backfire and harm your relationships (Egan, 1998). If I self-disclose too quickly with a client, I may be perceived as unprofessional and relating as a person and not a therapist. But, if I do not self-disclose early enough, some clients may terminate prematurely as they may not feel a "connection" with me on an intimate level. Maintaining the balance between appropriate and healthy self-disclosure versus inappropriate self-disclosure appears to be the key to developing healthy dating relationships and friendships.

Another advantage of self-disclosure is your observation of how the other person reacts to personal information. For example, you may disclose that you have always dreamed of living in the country and recently drove to a particular area. A superficial level of self-disclosure will then lead to a discussion of interests and future goals. If the person you are dating states that he fantasizes living in an uptown townhouse and being close to the local arts center then you will know that you two are not compatible in this area. You may not want a "green acres" relationship and this information may help you to make a decision about future dating with this person. You want to keep your self-disclosure superficial in the first few dates, but still disclose significant information.

Take the risk of disclosing more sensitive information as you have more dates, to further see how the other person reacts. For example, you may disclose that you have always dreamed of having a monogamous relationship with a committed partner. The expression of such a sensitive issue in a general manner allows the other person to express his own views. If the other person states he does not think men can be monogamous or he says nothing, then you know that he is not the person for you. A discussion of relationships and commitment does not mean you want such a relationship with that person. You are simply gaining information about his goals. You could also express an interest in children and having a child of your own to see how the other person reacts.

When I have shared this approach with clients, they have often had negative reactions. They have stated, "It sounds like you are testing the other person," "I don't think I could be so rational in dating someone," or "If you love someone, won't those things take care of themselves?" My answer has always been "No." Failure to discover such vital information during dating often leads to a relationship that is doomed to fail. You will also waste time dating a person with whom you are not compatible. This approach does not need to be similar to a job interview with that level of critique and harshness. You will need to be subtle and reveal these aspects about yourself at appropriate times.

Develop self-disclosure skills as you practice them in your dating. This is another reason to date many different partners without being sexual or committed to any of them. This process allows you to develop more effective social and communication skills. If you are uncomfortable, you can develop skills of self-disclosure by dating someone to whom you are not attracted. Remember that friendship dating is casual and there is no commitment involved. You can go on many first dates to develop dating and social skills.

A balance of appropriate self-disclosure will allow you to be more natural and spontaneous. One area of research has shown that people draw inferences about a person's personality based on the first few traits observed (see Jones and Davis, 1965; RoAnne, 1997). We tend to hold a personality "structure" in our minds and have constructs about how various personality traits go together. For example, we may perceive someone as neat and well groomed and then associate other traits with these two traits such as organized, polite, and intelligent. Our impression may be based on our past experience with neat and well-groomed individuals who also had these other traits and this assumption has likely been true most of the time.

You can use this information about inferences to your advantage. Knowing what traits are perceived as positive will allow you to approach the dating situation with a "marketing" mentality. You need to present yourself honestly, but also emphasize your best traits in the initial dates. This approach does not mean that you need to brag or appear overly confident. Your presentation traits would then be perceived negatively. Some traits to mention when first meeting someone are availability, promptness, dependability, neatness, good taste in clothing, politeness, and attentiveness (see Leary and Kowalski, 1990). Therapists are trained in these dynamics and are taught appropriate ways to present office space and advertising in order to provide a professional and caring impression. You can consult your friends about your mannerisms and dress for additional feedback or even hire a professional consultant for a "makeover." These approaches allow you to get your foot in the door, which is another successful marketing technique.

The impression-formation approach also has the potential to backfire and hurt your goal of making a good impression. You may attempt to create a positive impression by exaggerating some of your good qualities or even by appearing to be something you are not. For example, you may appear to be overly intellectual or sophisticated and may actually seem arrogant. You need to be yourself and allow your true positive qualities to emerge. This suggestion is usually regarded as overly simplistic but nothing could be more difficult. Portraying yourself in a genuine, yet positive manner is very difficult. You are "auditioning" for the part of potential dating partner and you are literally "on stage." You need to remember this on the first few dates or you will not be "chosen for the part." Acting does not always mean being fake and superficial. You are simply being the best you can be without putting on a facade or being deceptive.

Create a positive impression to your dating partners by disclosing areas of agreement. Balance theory is a social psychological theory that proposes a balance is created when two or three people agree on a topic, but imbalance is created when two agree but the third disagrees or when two people disagree (see Heider, 1958). This phenomenon is not foreign to most of us. You have probably been at a party or social gathering when two people were discussing a topic they agreed with and a third party expressed a contrary opinion. Such an interaction creates an uncomfortable imbalance that requires an effort to rectify. The eventual outcome is a compromise or agreement to disagree. Such a compromise may not have the opportunity to occur on a first date, so timing is crucial. Disclosing contrary opinions on the first date is not a good idea.

This approach does not suggest that you lie or appear fake and superficial. Just remember to speak up when you do agree and be very diplomatic when you do not. The main goal in the first few meetings is to create an attraction, not an argument or debate. You will have ample opportunity to express divergent opinions when you have developed this attraction and you have dated the person for several months. Many people think that being genuine and open means always expressing every thought and opinion. A salesperson would never focus on disagreement in the initial meetings and hope to make the sale. You need to remember your goals and reveal yourself in a genuine, yet positive, manner on the first few dates if you want to develop a positive impression and get more dates. Noone will ask you out again if you are not likable and pleasant. This is simply the way humans operate. We tend to seek out those things that are safe and pleasant and avoid those that are difficult and unpleasant.

Reasons to Avoid Sex on the First Date

1. *You avoid being used or exploited.* Many people will use a dating situation to cruise for sex. They are seeking a conquest and once sex occurs, this goal is accomplished and you are disposed of.
2. *You avoid using others.* Many people will go on a date with a person they do not plan to date again simply to use that person for sex. If you were honest, you have probably done this yourself.
3. *You avoid losing your objectivity.* Even if you tell yourself you can separate love and sex, most people cannot. When you become sexual with someone you really like, you risk losing your objectivity. You may then overlook areas where you are not compatible.
4. *You prevent unnecessary hurt.* When you open yourself up too quickly, you become vulnerable and can be harmed more easily than if you had moved more slowly and maintained appropriate boundaries.

5. *You prevent disillusionment and apathy with dating.* After going on multiple dates that end in sex and do not develop beyond this point, you risk becoming disillusioned and jaded with the dating experience. You may then give up on the goal of finding a healthy relationship and give in to promiscuity or avoidance.

6. *You avoid developing an easy reputation.* You risk developing a reputation as easy if you are having sexual encounters with people in the same social circle. You then risk attracting the wrong kind of person and may repel healthy dating partners.

7. *You avoid sabotaging a potentially healthy relationship.* Some people may misjudge you if you have sex too quickly even if they also consented to sex. Holding off communicates that you are interested in more than just sex.

8. *You maintain your morals and values.* By holding off on sex, you maintain healthy values of yourself and relationships.

9. *You avoid exposure to diseases and health risks.* Waiting to have sex increases the chance you will practice safe sex.

Chapter 17

Take Time to Get to Know Others

Give up the goal of true love. Love, if it is romantic, is never, strictly speaking, true. And, if it is not romantic, it is not true love.

James Ogilvy

You have now avoided the temptation to jump into bed and you are not shopping for china either (at least not yet!). You have found several men who are healthy and meet your list of compatible traits. Now you have to be patient and resist the temptation to rush into a hasty relationship. This stage is difficult as you are not used to feeling close to another man and there is a tendency to allow all of your "walls" to collapse as soon as you feel close. You are not yet in a relationship and you may confuse this pleasurable close feeling with love. M. Scott Peck, in *The Road Less Traveled,* discussed this tendency. He stated that people have a tendency to fall in love and seek a relationship with someone they feel close to regardless of whether this is the right person for them. You need to continue to date and go slowly as the newness wears off and you can learn more about your dating partner.

You may have also met some men who did not instantly "float your boat" but who had enough positive traits to keep you interested. Do not make a quick decision and risk losing a potentially healthy dating partner. Be open to going on second and third dates and do not allow yourself to close off your feelings too quickly. You can confuse feelings with facts and this is true for an initial negative reaction. You may resist doing this as you may think this is "stringing someone along." If the other person is healthy, there will be no expectations and he will respect your openness and willingness to remain objective. Going slow will also allow you to "weed out" those who want to have sex quickly. They will promptly disappear after one or two dates. You also need to continue to date even after you have found that "special person" with whom you think you can commit. You may have a tendency to act impulsively and realize later that you had made a quick decision. Your dating partner may become impatient with you, but stick to your plan. If your dating partner starts to become jealous or makes demands you will gain important information. Such a person would not be a healthy partner. His reaction will give you information about how you will be treated in a relationship.

This stage of dating will allow you to determine how secure your partner is about himself and the relationship. An individual who is intolerant of you continuing to date others until you are ready to commit will likely be jealous after you are in a relationship. You need to confront this issue and decide whether you want to be with someone who is insecure and jealous. Such an individual may actually want you to stop having single male friends after you have committed to a relationship.

Discussing the issue of jealousy may be very helpful as your dating partner may be buying into stereotypes of gay and bisexual men and may believe you cannot be faithful. This type of discussion may lead to a very frank conversation about your relationship and your sexual values. Your dating partner may have been hurt in past relationships and an open discussion can be very healing. Be careful not to judge your partner if he does become jealous and try to understand the beliefs and experiences that may have contributed to his reaction. Many men have also come from homes in which their parents divorced and married several times. This experience leads to the belief that relationships do not last. Again, open communication is the key to discovering more about one another.

Avoid the tendency to drop every other option when you think you have found the right person if you want to develop a healthy relationship. This reaction is normal but may actually keep you from finding your compatible mate. When you find someone who seems to have all the right characteristics, it is a relief to realize that your single life may finally be over. A strong tendency occurs to stop looking for other dating partners and settle into the relationship. Holding off on a commitment will allow you to continue to evaluate your partner as to whether you both are compatible. You lose some objectivity when you begin to believe that you have found your long-term partner, and are more likely to make some mistakes at this point. The biggest mistake is to overlook your partner's weaknesses. You may not discover these weaknesses or problems until you have been dating for some time. Holding off on a commitment and remaining objective will allow you to avoid overlooking these problem areas. If you start to invest all of your energy and time into this "new love," you may begin to stop the activities you were doing in order to meet other single men. If the relationship does not work out after a few months, you may lose your social network and may have to start over again to rebuild it. You may also realize that committing to one person is very frightening for you if you date only one person too soon. You may sabotage a healthy relationship if you become too anxious and you may push the other person away. The goal in developing a lasting relationship is to go slow so neither one of you gets overwhelmed. Building a gradual commitment is much more lasting than attempting to quickly create one. Resisting the temptation to leave the single world for the security of a relationship is vital if you are to remain objective and make a rational and healthy decision about a partner.

Chapter 18

Learn from Your Bad Dates

It is not the strongest of the species that survives, nor the most intelligent, but rather the one most responsive to change.

Charles Darwin

Taking breaks from the stress of dating can be very useful. Dating requires a great deal of time and energy. You will need to pause now and then to refresh yourself. Taking a break does not mean you jump into having casual sex. You still need to maintain your basic plan, but you can give yourself permission to pull back and regenerate. During my dating period, I often went on short vacations to wonderful places where I could hike and enjoy the scenery. Going alone allowed me to get away from everything and to enjoy being alone, another goal in my dating project. I visited several beautiful places and spent time walking and climbing mountains. I realized how valuable my solitary time was; it allowed me to be centered and relaxed with myself. I also used this time to do things with close friends and catch up on events in their lives. Several close friends at the time were going through similar events and it was refreshing to simply hang out and not feel pressured to date or have a boyfriend.

Take this time to discuss your dating experiences with other single friends and compare notes on what is working. My friends allowed me to discuss how my dating was going and they offered advice and suggestions. I still felt very awkward about dating and I obtained vital information from my single friends and gained additional support as I heard that they were having similar experiences. Their positive experiences offered me hope during the dry periods when nothing was happening. I gained much from having these single friends and this support at this time was invaluable in keeping up my momentum and optimism. They often gave me hope when I was about to give up, and kept me thinking positively and urged me to stay focused on having a relationship. They also offered friendship, which I needed, as I could not discuss my dating experiences with my family.

Take a moment to look back and pat yourself on the back for your progress. You need to remember that what you are doing takes a great deal of courage. Finding someone to simply have sex with is easy and requires very little skill. Going out on dates, developing social skills, maintaining several dating relationships, and handling many dating situations takes a great deal of energy. Remind yourself that you have chosen a difficult but rewarding path that will lead to a compatible partner. It is too easy to become discouraged and jaded. It is also easy to give up and believe you will never find a relationship. People often quit making positive changes just when they are about to succeed, not realizing that they were almost at their goal. You need to overcome the tendency to give up, and maintain hope and determination. It is my belief that people get what they want. You will eventually have a healthy relationship if you continue and do not give in to despair and hopelessness.

Be honest about your mistakes and use these as a growing and learning experience. Dating in a healthy manner will be a new opportunity for growth if you allow yourself to learn from your errors. No one has natural dating skills and you will become better at it the more you practice. If you allow yourself some room to grow you will discover that your telephone will start to ring off the hook with many invitations and offers. You may need to learn how to say "No!" Be patient and examine dates that did not go well and inventory your strengths and weaknesses. Avoid feeling bad or blaming the other person when things do not go well. This negative approach prevents learning and growth.

Make necessary changes to avoid repeating the mistakes you have made. I tend to talk too much about myself when I am nervous and meeting someone new. This type of behavior has been perceived as arrogance, but the opposite is actually true. I am actually insecure when meeting new people. Learning this aspect of my personality was painful and I still find myself slipping into this pattern on occasion. However, being honest and willing to be introspective allowed me to alter my unsuccessful behaviors.

Another way to learn about yourself in a social situation is to ask friends who are with you for their honest feedback. You will need to ask those friends you feel will be honest. Also, you will need to listen and not react defensively. Friends can be a great source of information if you are willing to use and apply their feedback. Group therapy can also be a way to gain more skills and understanding of your interpersonal patterns. Many therapists have groups with gay and bisexual men in order to develop increased social awareness and skills.

Affirmations are very helpful when you become discouraged. Avoid the tendency to blame yourself when a date does not go well or when you have no dating planned. At this point, you need to avoid total reliance on others for affirmation and work to develop your own positive self-concept. A date or a boyfriend does not define your worth as a person. Also, you may become nostalgic about the "good old days" when you could easily find someone to go to bed with. Dating healthy men is very different as healthy men are fewer and they are also discriminating. Remind yourself that you are engaging in a difficult task that will have great rewards. Tell yourself how attractive and sexy you are and repeat your affirmations daily. Tell yourself you are attracting healthy relationships and moving your life in a healthy direction. The result will be the development of a positive self-concept. You need this confidence to attract healthy dating partners and you need to prepare yourself for your next dating encounter. Hang in there even if you see no visible results, as much of the work in healthy dating is going on inside of you. The most difficult task is to change the way you think about yourself and others.

Affirmations

Negative statements that minimize or discount positive actions are putdowns. If you think positively about what you have done, though without exaggerating it, will improve your self-esteem. Statements you make to yourself about your strengths, talents, attributes, and accomplishments are called affirmations.

Choose any of the following statements for yourself:

I am a creative and successful person.
I am attractive and I naturally attract others to me.
I am sexy and I have powerful sexual energy.
I am creating my ideal career and job.
I have all of the money and means I need to accomplish my goals.
I trust my ability to overcome all of my barriers.

I love easily and others find me lovable.
Thinking positively about my future comes easily for me.
I am now creating healthy relationships in my life.
I am successful at earning money and achieving wealth.
I am a person others want to know and befriend.
I have endless energy and creativity.
I have great gifts to offer my fellow human beings.
I have a special contribution to offer others.
I work hard and persist in the face of difficulty.
I value the spirit in all living things.

Now write five of your own affirmations:

_____

_____

_____

_____

_____

Take time to just enjoy life as a single person. You may think that you would be happier if only you had a boyfriend. Nothing could be farther from the truth. Take a moment and make a list of all the things that are positive about being single and uncommitted. List all the opportunities, privileges, and activities you can engage in as a single person that you could not participate in if you were in a committed relationship. I have discovered that most of my free time is taken up with my partner since I have entered a relationship. I also used to take vacations alone to go hiking and sightseeing and my partner does not like these types of vacations. I have curtailed these activities, but also gained new ones. I do miss the freedom I had as a single person, though I enjoy being partnered as well. Reframing being single from a negative to a positive perspective will keep you in a productive frame of mind. There is nothing worse than being single and miserable while you are in the dating process. Take time to enjoy being single now because you will soon be in a relationship!

Do not stop socializing and going out during one of the break periods. You need to maintain a broad social network while you are single if you are going to have a broad selection of quality men. A lull in your dating is a perfect time to renew old acquaintances, attend parties at a new friend's home, check out new restaurants with close friends, and investigate other outlets such as singles groups or other social groups. You can also use this time to get out and market yourself and expand your network of support. You may find that many people are willing to help you if you are only in the right place at the right time. Always keep going even when you want to give up and you will find you are having a great time along the way. You may even regret having to curtail some of these activities once you find the right person.

Positive Aspects of Being Single

Examples: choosing how I spend my time; decorating my place the way I like; sleeping in with no interruptions.

1. _____
2. _____
3. _____
4. _____
5. _____
6. _____
7. _____
8. _____
9. _____
10. _____
11. _____
12. _____
13. _____
14. _____
15. _____
16. _____
17. _____
18. _____
19. _____
20. _____
21. _____
22. _____
23. _____
24. _____
25. _____
26. _____

110 FINDING A LOVER FOR LIFE

27. _____

28. _____

29. _____

30. _____

Chapter 19

Don't Give Up When You Get Discouraged

There's always something to suggest you'll never be who you want to be. Your choice is to take it or keep on moving.

Phylicia Rashad

Be careful not to become discouraged. Healthy dating is often a long and tedious process that has few immediate rewards. You will need to work to avoid the temptation to become discouraged. Many of my clients have expressed how different and unpleasant they found healthy dating. You will find yourself becoming more discriminating about the men you date and will be eliminating dating partners from your list of potential partners. Expect times when you have dated a great deal for several months and have not yet found the right match, or times when you are dating several men and having a good time but you realize that you have not found the right person. These times are frustrating and can be stressful. Keeping your focus on your final goals will keep you from being discouraged.

Remind yourself that there is no hurry to find the right person. People tend to make stupid mistakes or impulsive decisions when they are in a hurry. Think about the relationship with this person five and ten years from now. If you and your partner are not compatible, the relationship will either cease or you will be miserable. Plan for permanence, not a separation. You are looking for that unique person who shares your vision in life, not just a person who is fun to be with. You would not settle for a car or house you did not want just because you were tired of looking, so keep up the search for a partner until you find who you want. Plenty of guys are out there, but there are only a few will match the qualities you are seeking.

Keep your life as interesting as possible. Remember that you are not putting your life on hold as a single person and that you are continuing to develop an interesting and exciting relationship with yourself. Do not limit yourself to dating only. Continue to pursue your own interests and friendships, which will make this period interesting. The pursuit of other interests will also keep you in a healthy emotional state and you will be less vulnerable to attracting unhealthy partners. Avoid becoming needy when you get discouraged; certain types will pick up on your neediness. Stay confident and happy even when you are struggling with maintaining healthy dating. Tell people the positives about dating when they ask and be careful not to complain. Patience will pay off in the long run.

Make a list of pleasurable activities as a reminder of your goals when you are feeling discouraged. Such activities include getting a massage, going to a movie, shopping, having a special meal, or using a personal trainer. These activities will boost your mood and keep you from feeling depressed. Encourage yourself and keep a song in your heart. Tell yourself that you are being prepared and that your partner is being prepared at that same moment. Reinforce this belief by reminding yourself and staying in a state of anticipation. Trust the universal energy that is drawing you and your partner together. Visualize your relationship to stay focused and open to your perfect partner. This approach may seem simplistic but it works.

Continue to get feedback from your support team and call them when you are discouraged. This type of social support can allow you to remain positive even when you feel that you are failing. You also need to remind yourself that being in a relationship will not solve any other problems you are currently experiencing. Many people believe that "two can live cheaper then one," and they look for a relationship to offer them financial security. The opposite is actually true. Couples tend to travel more, buy houses, furniture, and decorations.

Remind yourself that being in a relationship will not solve the frustrations you have as a single person. You will have the same and many more challenges when you are partnered. There will still be periods of little or no sexual activity, as your partner may travel or work away from home, and you will have occasional feelings of loneliness. You and your partner may face major life changes such as children, relocation, or illness. Idealizing a relationship will only set you up to be unhappy and dissatisfied when you are in a relationship. You will then idealize and fantasize about your "happy single days" when you had no problems. Remember, not needing a relationship to be happy or complete is a goal that will make you happier once you find your mate. Continue to develop the positive aspect of a single life and tell yourself that you will be happy regardless of the outcome of your relationship goals. Not needing a relationship to be happy or complete is a trait that will actually make you more attractive to a healthy partner.

Chapter 20

Remember to Stay Focused

There is nothing so easy but that it becomes difficult when you do it reluctantly.

Terence

Persistence is the major factor in succeeding at any project, but it can also be the main reason for failure. I have seen this dynamic in clients who quit making positive changes right at the moment they were about to achieve success. The main reason for this tendency to give up is that many of the behavioral patterns that prevent growth are well entrenched and a great deal of diligent effort is required to develop new patterns. The analogy I like to use is the sledgehammer and brick wall. The first 100 hammer hits with the hammer may only make a small dent, but the wall is weakening. You never know when you will hit the wall and it will come crumbling down.

Distractions and barriers to your goals will present themselves and your persistence will pay off. Short- and long-term goals are very important. You need to perceive progress to maintain your desire to complete your task. Also, most tasks take much longer than planned. When I was in graduate school I had a general rule that allowed me to stay focused: "Everything takes at least four times longer that you plan." This approach allowed me to avoid getting discouraged, which nearly happened several times. Your dating project will take time and consistent effort and patience will allow you to persist until you achieve your goal. Persistence is the power that allowed erosion to create the Grand Canyon over millions of years. The Himalayas were not created in one great collision of India and the Asian continent. These gigantic mountains developed over millions of years. The gradual and persistent pressure from the merging of the two continents pushed the mountains up from the flat plains. This same principle will work for you in both finding the right partner and persisting when you are in a relationship.

Take a moment to again list your goals. You may want to set new ones based on the information you have gathered from your dating experiences. Some sample goals are to develop new interests and hobbies, maintain an exercise program, travel and see more places, take an adult learning class to broaden your knowledge, learn a second or third language, or volunteer at a nonprofit agency (see chapter's end). Your decision to continue to develop yourself and your personality allow you to enjoy the "here and now." Too often we see ourselves happy in the future, rather than working on being happy today. Whatever happens with your dating plan, have a plan to enjoy the present. I learned to do many new and interesting things when I was single. These same skills have allowed me to stay satisfied and happy in my current situation as a partnered person.

The skill of being happy with what you have at the moment is probably the most difficult one you will ever develop. We sing a song at my church every Sunday after communion called "It Is Well with My Soul." A man who had just been informed that his wife and children had died wrote the song. He wrote the song in a period of his life when acceptance of his reality must have been very difficult. This song advocates an excellent goal whether or not you are religious.

My involvement in Alcoholics Anonymous also taught me to live in the day and take "One day at a time." Learning to enjoy the moment will allow you to weather many of life's storms. Once you are in a relationship, many days will be difficult. Learning to enjoy the moment while you are single will allow you to endure the struggles you face now and in the future. Remember that you are developing the kind of person you want to find. These goals will allow you to continue to develop your personality and make you into an interesting and attractive individual. You will have many interesting topics to talk about when you do meet people and go on dates. You will have a life and will be growing and developing rather than waiting for a relationship to begin your life. You may also discover many things about yourself you never knew. These discoveries can lead to more growth as you address uncharted areas. You will be meeting people and developing social skills, which will further develop your social network and greatly increase your chances of finding a mate. You will become much more attractive and interesting, which will attract others.

Self-Esteem Goals Checklist

Self-esteem occurs when we practice positive behaviors and seek to improve ourselves. Check off the positive behaviors you will develop to create a positive self-concept:

_____ Start an exercise program
_____ Develop a new hobby
_____ Make new friends
_____ Try a new haircut
_____ Go on an exotic vacation
_____ Learn a new language
_____ Take an adult learning class
_____ Take a class in public speaking
_____ Join a church group
_____ Attend a fund-raiser
_____ Learn a new skill
_____ Do something daring or exciting (e.g., hang gliding)
_____ Update your wardrobe
_____ Get a massage
_____ Join a support group
_____ Join a new social group
_____ Attend a seminar or workshop

Chapter 21

Let the Relationship Happen

I define love thus: The will to extend one's self for the purpose
of nurturing one's own or another's spiritual growth.

M. Scott Peck

Unfortunately, most gay men know only two modes of relating to
other men: having sex with them or rejecting them. This faulty socialization handicaps them as they seek to develop healthy relationships.
Another handicap is the lack of societal support and role models in
demonstrating healthy same-sex relationships. Many gay and bisexual men have learned how to relate to one another in bars and they
tend to sexualize every encounter with other men. This type of interaction is called "cruising." Gay and bisexual men have also learned
how to reject those who do not fit the package of "gay attractiveness."
This negative interaction is a repetition of the same faulty socialization that initially handicapped gay and bisexual men.

A relationship is a creation. No one is born with the skills to develop and maintain a healthy relationship. Most people have very
busy lives and the relationship may take a backseat to other activities.
Spending time together is one way of creating closeness in your relationship. Other ways to enhance your relationship are attending
counseling together, developing better communication skills, attending a relationship workshop, attending a couples Bible study, and
reading books on communication skills. Much time is spent to develop skills in other areas, yet little is devoted to develop a relationship. An investment of time and effort now will pay off, as you will be
prepared when difficulties occur in the future.

A relationship is a mutual process. I have found that my partner
and I often have very different perspectives on the same issue. The
process of listening and seeking middle ground is often excruciating

and painful. I am very surprised just how different our views can be at times. The task to let go of my own perspective and seek to understand his views is difficult. However, the outcome of this process is always fruitful, and I have often found a new and different way viewpoint. At these times, I am reminded of the many reasons I found him attractive and exciting in the first place. As an individual, I have grown a great deal from these situations.

Forming a lasting union from two different lives is a monumental task. Many times we associate conflict with problems in the relationship. Conflict is a natural part of any relationship. Careers, money, future goals, children, and other issues surface over differences. Set a goal to work very hard to make the relationship last. It may seem easier to give up and walk away when difficulties emerge, or to tell yourself that you will be happier with someone else. However, the same conflicts will occur with another partner. Many of our unresolved issues from childhood and past relationships surface during controversy and this can be a time of great growth and pain. Allow yourself to welcome these encounters, to work through such issues as control, power, and individuality in a close relationship. Face contention head-on when it occurs.

The most important ingredient in creating a lasting relationship is selflessness. I have found that this is the trait I lack the most in my relationship. Too often I think of my needs first and focus only on how the relationship affects me. I need to work very hard to let go of my own agenda and open myself up to my partner's needs. My selfishness is associated with my difficulty with trust and with my need to be in control. I have learned that I need to let go of this control to trust my partner. With trust, I can then seek to please him and blend with him in a way that leads to our mutual growth. This process has involved great loss and letting go as I have sought to be selfless. Selflessness is the expression of unconditional love. I believe that receiving this type of love is our deepest desire. As I am able to let go and release myself to my love for my partner, I find I am at peace and am content. The feeling of unconditional love has no substitute. As I experience selflessness and loss of my own desires, I also experience my partner's unconditional love.

Life has no guarantees and there is no perfect relationship. You will find your ideal mate only if you allow your life to develop naturally. Love has a way of bringing peace into every situation. You and your partner will find many changes in your health, career, financial situation, and families. These changes will occur in many unpredictable ways. Love will allow you and your partner to have a point of constancy throughout all of these changes and you will create an eternal and lasting love. This love will offer you both a place of refuge during the many storms of life. Many people do not recognize this benefit of commitment. You will find that your relationship has a life and identity of its own. This is the great secret of love.

Stages of Healthy Dating

Meeting

You may see the first date as a romantic encounter. This is a mistake. The healthiest way to approach the first date is to consider this a meeting in which there are no expectations for future dating. This approach can prevent hurt feelings and unnecessary rejection. You need to go on many dates to learn more about yourself and the type of person you are comfortable around. If you remove the pressure of the first meeting to be a romantic encounter it will be a more pleasant experience. Too often our own expectations become the problem and keep us from getting what we want. No date or meeting is wasted if you view it as a learning experience, and will allow you to develop better dating skills. You need to remember that "love at first sight" rarely happens and when it does it rarely leads to positive results.

Friendship Stage

You may decide to date again if the first meeting went well. You are getting to know the other person and evaluating whether you and he are compatible. No expectations for any long-term commitments exist at this time and the dating is relaxed and casual. Friendship dating is a lost art, but a very valuable activity, and a great way to develop a resource of other single friends. When you hold off on having sex and the dating relationship does not continue, you have then gained a new friend. Always be direct during this stage. Do not lead someone on and do not "blow off" a dating partner. If you decide not to date someone, do not make plans with him for later. If he persists, offer him a date four or five months in advance and state that you are very busy. Be direct that you do not perceive the possibility of a romantic relationship if the person continues to persist. Directness usually is respected, while avoidance is perceived as rude.

Nonexclusive Dating Stage

Even if you really like the other person, it is a good idea to hold off emotionally and continue to date others. This experience will allow you to remain objective and truly sort out how you feel about dating one person. You can also compare how compatible you are with several partners and see which traits you like best in a romantic partner. If you are honest with all of those involved, no one will be hurt.

Exclusive Dating Stage

Now you are ready to start looking at china patterns. When you are ready to select one person to date exclusively, discuss this decision with your partner to evaluate if this is a mutual decision. If you do not discuss your decision, you risk making assumptions that can later come back to harm the relationship. You and your partner can now set boundaries such as making a monogamous commitment.

Precommitment Stage

After dating for a period of time, you and your partner can begin to discuss the possibility of commitment, a stage similar to engagement if you were to become legally married. No full commitment has been made and the possibility of choosing to end the relationship is still a viable option. This stage is a good time to examine your mutual compatibility. Precommitment or premarital counseling is also recommended at this stage.

Commitment Stage

At this stage, you and your partner make a mutual decision to be committed. Your commitment may take the form of cohabiting or sharing some life goal. Discussions of the future, children, demographics, and other relationship issues becomes more serious as the committed relationship becomes a reality. This stage can be very euphoric, but it can also be very stressful and tense.

Marriage/Civil Union Stage

Marriage for lesbians and gay men has been legally denied in most states. However, we can choose to celebrate our union in a spiritual manner. We can also tie our lives together legally in the form of a living trust and legal guardianship. Same-sex couples do not need to buy into the oppression of the society and miss out on the joy of a celebration of their love together. This experience can be very rewarding for you, your partner, and your families and friends.

Negotiating Differences Stage

After a formal commitment has been made, the task of compromising and accepting differences begins. The blending of two lives can be very tense. The goal at this stage is negotiating and blending your many differences. The couple attempts to understand and accept each other's differing styles, attitudes, and backgrounds, and integrate into a combined life together.

Conflict-Resolution Stage

The conflict-resolution stage can be very emotional as each person strives to meet his own needs in the relationship while learning how to meet the needs of his partner. Many mistakes occur at this point and a great deal of forgiveness and gentleness is required to survive. Many unresolved relationship issues emerge at this stage and this can be a very enlightening process.

Acceptance Stage

The couple has attained acceptance of each other's differences at this stage. They have come to appreciate these differences as strengths rather than obstacles. They have also achieved a balance in their personal and professional lives so that no one area suffers. The relationship is a place of refuge where they can retreat from their busy lives. Confrontation and honesty allows for continued growth.

Chapter 22

Keep the Lover You Find
by Continuing to Grow

Some luck lies in not getting what you thought you wanted but getting what you have, which once you have got it you may be smart enough to see it is what you would have wanted had you known.

Garrison Keillor

Unfortunately, you will forget all the healthy lessons you have learned about dating and relationships the moment you fall in love. All of us tend to become blind when we are infatuated and we tend to overlook the faults and problems in our beloved. You will be fine if you simply remember that this is normal and that this blindness will wear off. It usually takes about four to six months. This is usually the period of most break-ups. The couple who was initially "madly in love," starts to see all the quirks and drawbacks of a relationship with each other. Remember to keep both your love and your objectivity and you will survive both the initial infatuation and the subsequent crisis stage of your new relationship.

Keep the man you find. After you have worked this hard to attain a healthy relationship, you need to keep up the same skills and goals you had when you were single. You also need to learn more skills such as communication and conflict resolution. The initial stage of a committed relationship is often called the honeymoon stage, as the couple is enjoying each other. Very little conflict exists at this stage. However, it is brief and controversy will soon emerge. You will learn that you are two different people with different tastes and interests, and that you both also have unpleasant habits and pet peeves. Living together presents many challenges and opportunities for growth.

Due to past socialization, two men in a relationship will naturally be competitive. This competition is the source of many conflicts for male couples. Men are socialized in our culture to dominate, to be in control, and to lead. Admitting a wrong is not a natural thing for most men to do. Men feel "one down" when admitting they are at fault. The strongest tendency among men is to "fight to the finish." This behavioral pattern is partly genetic and partly learned. However, you can recognize your tendency to fight and win and avoid needless conflict.

Men are also not socialized to communicate their feelings and needs. This type of communication is seen as weak and feminine in our culture. Men grow up inhibiting and avoiding emotional expression as a part of being male. This tendency to suppress emotions is also expressed in same-sex relationships. Many people incorrectly believe that a good relationship is one in which conflict does not occur. An individual with this belief may hold in his feelings until he becomes resentful or explodes. The person's partner may then perceive him as overreacting and may not understand his feelings. Men are especially prone to walk away at this point and perceive that the partner is incapable of getting along. You will need to express your feelings and listen to your partner's feelings in order to succeed in a relationship.

Open communication and acknowledgment of differences is essential to creating a lasting relationship. It is too easy to avoid a problem or difficulty with the hope it will work itself out. The ability of a couple to directly address problems in the relationship will allow the relationship to grow from difficulties rather than deteriorate. Communication allows each person to share his deepest fears and concerns within an environment of acceptance and understanding. Such an environment is difficult to achieve, especially between two men who have not learned to share on such an emotional level. This type of relationship allows a great deal of emotional healing to occur. Open communication also allows for healthy discussion and problem solving. Avoidance of problems leads only to emotions building up and erupting in destructive ways. One partner eventually explodes, acts impulsively, or suddenly leaves the relationship. Many couples find that they cannot do this on their own; a therapist or coach can be of great help at these times.

Conflict avoidance is also responsible for domestic violence (see Vivian and Langhinrichsen-Rohling, 1996). Relationship violence in the gay community is a hidden problem (see Miller, 1996). Many people do not take domestic partner violence seriously, especially when it occurs between two men. Men do not readily perceive themselves as victims and fail to report the violence and assault (see Letellier, 1996). They may perceive that the legal authorities will not treat them with respect or may actually demean them. The belief in our society is that "two men are supposed to fight it out," and that this leads to a successful resolution. Many men engaged in physical violence as children and became friends with the boys they attacked. Gay and bisexual men may harbor anger related to rejection from society. They may direct this anger at their partners. Domestic violence is high in minority populations for this reason. Learn to deal with anger. This is essential if you and your partner are to remain together and avoid violence.

Many gay and bisexual men have had fathers who were physically or verbally abusive (Letellier, 1996). This issue can cause problems in relating openly with your partner. You may have difficulty trusting your partner, as you may fear he will use your disclosure to harm you. You may fear his rejection if you share your feelings. Your unresolved abuse trauma will lead you to distance yourself from your partner. When you experience conflict, you may have a tendency to withdraw and not communicate your feelings. This withdrawal may be misperceived as rejection, which may lead to more problems. The result of such a relationship pattern is that you may come to believe that men are not trustworthy and then act to fulfill you own self-destructive beliefs.

Learn to recognize when you are feeling insecure or vulnerable in your relationship. Risk communicating these feelings to your partner. Tell him about your past abuse and process this trauma with him. Allow him to offer support and ask questions. Be patient with him if he does not understand immediately. Individuals who have not been abused do not readily understand the long-term effects of such abuse. Your partner actually may be blaming himself for many of your reactions and he may become defensive.

Integrating your lifestyle into your partner's will be a continuous goal as you form your relationship. You may have only considered the benefits of being in a relationship when you made the decision to commit to your partner and may have failed to recognize that there are many compromises in a successful relationship. You both must be willing to give up some things such as work hours, free time, spending time with others or family, certain activities, or finances in order to make the relationship work. The tendency is to view sacrifices as unhealthy in our self-oriented culture. Our culture seems to emphasize placing personal happiness above the importance of family or relationships.

Making sacrifices is especially crucial if you and your partner decide to adopt children. Children demand a great deal from their parents and this is a natural and normal process. Committed individuals who are also parents will find that they have difficulty meeting their own needs and their children's and partners' needs. The key to success in this situation is communication and compromise. Compromise means that no one person gets all of what he wants but each gets some of what he wants. You may have disappointment at this stage as you realize that you must give up some things in order to have a successful relationship and family. Balance is the goal to meeting your needs, your partner's needs, and your children's needs (if this is your situation). Workshops and couple counseling will aid in this process.

Premarital or precommitment counseling is very useful when you and your partner are considering moving in together and making a commitment. Several books address communication skills for couples and these are also useful. Simply learning a few skills may make all the difference in gaining an ability to communicate and resolve conflict. Too many relationships end needlessly when the couples simply fail to use appropriate communication skills. They then perceive that the conflict is impossible to resolve and they give up. Much more could be said about this stage of relationship formation, but that would require another book.

Well, here you are at the end of the book. I hope you have gained a new understanding of how to date successfully and find a healthy relationship. You have likely been surprised by many of the statements in this book. Perhaps you have also taken an honest look at yourself and have learned a great deal. You have gained many new skills and the task now is to use these skills. You will discover much about yourself if you are honest and painstaking. Allow your situation at this time to be a point of growth and departure as you venture into a new land of healthy dating. You will discover many new delights and surprises if you are open to them. You will find yourself on the path to a lasting relationship, and will soon find your partner waiting and smiling. Remember that you have the ability to create a healthy relationship and attract your perfect partner. Visualize your success and move your entire being in that direction. Your happiness is only a few steps away!

Ways to Ensure Legal Status of Your Marital Relationship

1. *Legal guardianship*
2. *Will and testament*
3. *Living trust*
4. *Beneficiary*
5. *Estate*
6. *Move to Vermont*

Appendix

Dating Journal

Use this journal to take notes as you read through the book or as you are dating. Good luck on your journey to finding a lover for life!

1. Stop running from commitment.

_____
_____
_____
_____
_____

2. Have a plan to find your man.

_____
_____
_____
_____
_____

3. Face your fears of getting close.

_____
_____
_____
_____
_____

4. Don't try to succeed alone.

_____
_____
_____
_____
_____

5. Prepare yourself emotionally.

_____

_____

_____

_____

_____

6. Let go of old entanglements.

_____

_____

_____

_____

_____

7. Make room for a relationship.

_____

_____

_____

_____

_____

8. Make a Compatibility Inventory.

_____

_____

_____

_____

_____

9. Decide whom you want to be.

_____

_____

_____

_____

_____

10. Develop your values and standards.

_____

_____

_____

11. Invest in your dating plan.

12. Deal with failures and setbacks.

13. Watch out for the hidden dangers.

14. Keep up your momentum.

15. Gather information on the date.

16. Open up and let others in.

_____

_____

_____

_____

_____

17. Take time to get to know others.

_____

_____

_____

_____

_____

18. Learn from your bad dates.

_____

_____

_____

_____

_____

19. Don't give up when you get discouraged.

_____

_____

_____

_____

_____

20. Remember to stay focused.

_____

_____

_____

_____

21. Let the relationship happen.

_____

_____

_____

22. Keep the lover you find by continuing to grow.

Bibliography

Asch, S.E. (1946). Forming impressions of personality. *Journal of Abnormal and Social Psychology, 41,* 258-290.

Ayers, T. and Brown, P. (1994). *The essential guide to lesbian and gay weddings.* San Francisco: Harper.

Berg, J.H. and Peplau, L.A. (1982). Loneliness: The relationship of self-disclosure and androgyny. *Personality and Social Psychology Bulletin, 8,* 624-630.

Berzon, B. (1990). *Permanent partners.* New York: Penguin Books.

Burns, D. (1980). *Intimate connections.* New York: Penguin Books.

Caldwell, M.A. and Peplau, L.A. (1982). Sex differences in same-sex friendships. *Sex Roles, 8,* 721-731.

Carnes, P. (1983). *Out of the shadows.* Minneapolis: CompCare Publishers.

Carnes, P. (1985). *Don't call it love.* New York: Bantam Books.

Chelune, G., Sultan, F., and Williams, C. (1980). Loneliness, self-disclosure, and interpersonal effectiveness. *Journal of Counseling Psychology, 27,* 462-468.

Clark, D. (1987). *Loving someone gay.* Berkeley: Celestial Arts.

Davis, M. and Franzoi, S. (1986). Adolescent loneliness, self-disclosure, and private self-consciousness: A longitudinal investigation. *Journal of Personality and Social Psychology, 51,* 595-608.

Dean, R. B. and Richardson, H. (1964). Analysis of MMPI profiles of forty college-educated overt male homosexuals. *Journal of Consulting Psychology, 28,* 483-486.

Dion, K., Berscheid, E., and Walster, E. (1972). What is beautiful is good. *Journal of Personality and Social Psychology, 24,* 285-290.

Driggs, J. H. and Finn, S. E. (1991). *Intimacy between men.* New York: Plume Publishers.

Egan, G. (1998). *The skilled helper.* Pacific Grove, CA: Brooks/Cole Publishing Company.

Erikson, E. (1968). *Identity: Youth and crisis.* New York: W. W. Norton and Company.

Forstein, M. (1988). Homophobia: An overview. *Psychiatric Annals, 18,* 33-36.

Franzoi, S. and Davis, M. (1985). Adolescent self-disclosure and loneliness: Private self-consciousness and parental influences. *Journal of Personality and Social Psychology, 48,* 768-780.

Freedman, M. (1971). *Homosexuality and psychological functioning.* Belmont, CA: Brooks/Cole.

Freud, A. (1936). *The ego and the mechanisms of defense.* New York: International University Press.

Gibran, K. (1923). *The Prophet.* New York: Random House.

Goffman, E. (1959). *The presentation of self in everyday life.* New York: Doubleday Anchor.

Gouldner, A. (1960). The norm of reciprocity: A preliminary statement. *American Sociological Review, 25,* 161-178.

Heider, F. (1958). *The psychology of interpersonal relations.* New York: Wiley.

Helgeson, V., Shaver, P., and Dyer, M. (1987). Prototypes of intimacy and distance in same-sex and opposite-sex relationships. *Journal of Personal and Social Relationships, 4,* 195-233.

Hendrix, H. (1988). *Getting the love you want.* New York: Harper & Row Publishers.

Herek, G. M. (1984). Beyond "homophobia": A social psychological perspective on attitudes towards lesbians and gay men. *Journal of Homosexuality, 10*(1/2), 2-17.

Isay, R. A. (1989). *Being homosexual.* New York: Farrar, Straus, and Giroux.

Jones, E. and Davis, K. (1965). From acts to dispositions: The attribution process in person perception. In L. Berkowitz (Ed.), *Advances in experimental social psychology* (Vol. 7, pp. 219-266). New York: Academic Press.

Jourard, S. (1959). Self-disclosure and other cathexis. *Journal of Abnormal and Social Psychology, 59,* 428-431.

Jourard, S. (1971). *The transparent self.* New York: Van Nostrand.

Keyes, K. (1979). *A conscious person's guide to relationships.* Marina del Rey, CA: DeVorss and Company.

Leary, M. and Kowalski, R. (1990). Impression management: A literature review. *Psychological Bulletin, 107,* 34-47.

Letellier, P. (1996). Gay and bisexual male domestic violence victimization: Challenges to feminist theory and responses to violence. In L. Hamberger and C. Renzetti (Eds.), *Domestic partner abuse* (pp. 1-22). New York: Springer Publishing Company.

Mellody, P. (1992). *Facing love addiction.* New York: HarperCollins.

Miller, S. (1996). Expanding the boundaries: Toward a more inclusive and integrated study of intimate violence. In L. Hamberger and C. Renzetti (Eds.), *Domestic partner abuse* (pp. 191-212). New York: Springer Publishing Company.

Miller, W. G. (1963). Characteristics of homosexually-involved incarcerated females. *Journal of Consulting Psychology, 27,* 277.

Ogilvy, J. 1995). *Living without a goal.* New York: Doubleday Dell Publishing Group, Inc.

Ohlson, E. L. and Wilson, M. (1974). Differentiating female homosexuals from female heterosexuals by use of the MMPI. *Journal of Sex Research, 10,* 308-315.

Peck, M. S. (1978). *The road less traveled.* New York: Simon and Schuster.

Ray, S. (1976). *I deserve love.* Millbrae, CA: Les Femmes.

Ray, S. (1980). *Loving relationships.* Berkeley: Celestial Arts.

Reis, H., Senchak, M., and Solomon, B. (1985). Sex differences in the intimacy of social interaction: Further examination of potential explanations. *Journal of Personality and Social Psychology, 48,* 1204-1217.

Rich, H. (1993). *Get married now.* Holbrook, MA: Bob Adams.

RoAnne, S. (1997). *What do I say next?* New York: Warner Books.

Saghir, M. T. and Robins, E. (1973). *Male and female homosexuality: A comprehensive investigation.* Baltimore, MD: Williams and Wilkins.

Simring, S. K. and Simring, S. (1990). *The compatibility quotient.* New York: Fawcett Columbine.

Smith, J. (1988). Psychopathology, homosexuality, and homophobia. In M. W. Ross (Eds.), *Psychopathology and psychotherapy in homosexuality* (pp. 59-74). Binghamton, NY: The Haworth Press, Inc.

Tessina, T. (1989). *Gay relationships.* New York: Tarcher/Putnam.

Vivian, D. and Langhinrichsen-Rohling, J. (1996). Are bi-directionally violent violent couples mutually victimized? A gender-sensitive comparison. In L. Hamberger and C. Renzetti (Eds.), *Domestic partner abuse* (pp. 23-53). New York: Springer Publishing Company.

Worthy, M., Gary, A., and Kahn, G. (1969). Self-disclosure as an exchange process. *Journal of Personality and Social Psychology, 13,* 59-63.

Index

Abuse/trauma. *See also* Homophobia; Rejection
  and impairment of relationship skills, 31, 33, 127
  and reenactment in sadomasochistic sex, 81
  and verbal abuse, 30
Addiction, 83. *See also* Love addiction; Sexual compulsivity/addiction
  and destruction of a relationship, 32
  as a potential danger in dating, 52
Affairs/cheating, 64
Affirmations for relationships, 107
AIDS. *See also* HIV infection; HIV status
  and awareness of "safe sex," 3, 4
  and the gay community's response to, 3
  as a political issue, 4
Alcohol and substance abuse, 83. *See also* Addiction
Alcoholics Anonymous, 116
Attraction
  and attracting who we are, 57
  and enmeshment, 82
  to married gay and bisexual men, 77
"Attractiveness stereotyping," 52

Balance theory, 97, 98
Bisexual men married to women, 76, 77
Buscaglia, Leo, 39

Caesars of Rome, 81
"Cinderella complex," 32
"Circuit parties," 83, 84
Civil union, 11, 122
Cocaine use, 83

Codependency, 37, 78, 82. *See also* Love addiction
Cohabiting relationship, 10
Commitment
  to finding a partner, 10, 122
  holding off on, 102, 103
  the importance in a lasting relationship of, 10
Committed/marital relationship, 11
Communication, 126
Compatibility
  and success in a lasting relationship, 49
  as a tool for making healthy decisions, 111
Compatibility Inventory, 49, 50, 51, 55, 565
Conflict. *See also* Relationship(s)
  and resolving differences, 123, 126
  as a testing ground, 54
  and violence, 126, 127
"Cruising," 119

"Daddy" types, 79
Dance party phenomenon, 83, 84
Darwin, Charles, 105
Dating. *See also* Relationship(s)
  coping with setbacks and discouragement while, 86, 111
  and creating a positive impression, 97, 98
  to develop friendships, 11, 121
  going slow while, 103
  healthy, 7, 106, 111
  and investing time, money and energy, 43, 44, 68, 69, 85
  as a rational exercise, 50, 51, 54
  and self-disclosure, 91, 93-96
  and social skills, 67-68

141

Order Your Own Copy of
This Important Book for Your Personal Library!

FINDING A LOVER FOR LIFE
A Gay Man's Guide to Finding a Lasting Relationship

_____ in hardbound at $29.95 (ISBN: 1-56023-356-7)

_____ in softbound at $14.95 (ISBN: 1-56023-357-5)

COST OF BOOKS_____

OUTSIDE USA/CANADA/
MEXICO: ADD 20%_____

POSTAGE & HANDLING_____
(US: $4.00 for first book & $1.50
for each additional book)
Outside US: $5.00 for first book
& $2.00 for each additional book)

SUBTOTAL_____

in Canada: add 7% GST_____

STATE TAX_____
(NY, OH & MIN residents, please
add appropriate local sales tax)

FINAL TOTAL____
(If paying in Canadian funds,
convert using the current
exchange rate, UNESCO
coupons welcome.)

❑ **BILL ME LATER:** ($5 service charge will be added)
(Bill-me option is good on US/Canada/Mexico orders only;
not good to jobbers, wholesalers, or subscription agencies.)

❑ Check here if billing address is different from
shipping address and attach purchase order and
billing address information.

Signature_____

❑ **PAYMENT ENCLOSED: $_____**

❑ **PLEASE CHARGE TO MY CREDIT CARD.**

❑ Visa ❑ MasterCard ❑ AmEx ❑ Discover
❑ Diner's Club ❑ Eurocard ❑ JCB

Account # _____

Exp. Date_____

Signature_____

Prices in US dollars and subject to change without notice.

NAME_____

INSTITUTION_____

ADDRESS_____

CITY_____

STATE/ZIP_____

COUNTRY_____ COUNTY (NY residents only)_____

TEL_____ FAX_____

E-MAIL_____

May we use your e-mail address for confirmations and other types of information? ❑ Yes ❑ No
We appreciate receiving your e-mail address and fax number. Haworth would like to e-mail or fax special
discount offers to you, as a preferred customer. **We will never share, rent, or exchange your e-mail address
or fax number.** We regard such actions as an invasion of your privacy.

Order From Your Local Bookstore or Directly From
The Haworth Press, Inc.
10 Alice Street, Binghamton, New York 13904-1580 • USA
TELEPHONE: 1-800-HAWORTH (1-800-429-6784) / Outside US/Canada: (607) 722-5857
FAX: 1 800 895-0582 / Outside US/Canada: (607) 722-6362
E-mail: getinfo@haworthpressinc.com
PLEASE PHOTOCOPY THIS FORM FOR YOUR PERSONAL USE.
www.HaworthPress.com

BOF00